# Do-It-Yourself
# Projects
# for
# Bowhunters

BOWHUNTING PRESERVATION ALLIANCE

# Do-It-Yourself Projects for Bowhunters

## Peter Fiduccia
### and
## Leo Somma

Skyhorse Publishing

# ACKNOWLEDGMENTS

To my wife Beth for understanding the time commitment needed to build these projects, to write them up, and the time away from home, as many of these projects were built at our farm. As with my first book, 25 *Projects for Outdoorsmen,* she benefited from a few projects which are used in our present home. I'll love her forever.

To my sons Matthew and Michael, both successful and trouble-free children, who afforded me the time to spend away from the family. I am also grateful that they both have shown an interest in hunting, a sport that we can enjoy together and treasure for a lifetime. To my cousin Peter, for another chance and whose confidence allowed me to coauthor a second book. As with our first, we were able to share our passion of the outdoors while building these useful and practical projects to use at our family farm, deer cabin, and homes. To Jay for sponsoring the book to be shared by the youth involved in the world of archery.

*Leo Somma, August 2012*

To my wife Kate for her unwavering support in any undertaking I venture to do. Without her strength, love, and professional skills I would not be where I am today. And to my son Cody, who makes me more proud of his many achievements with each passing day. I love you both more than words can describe. And to Leo for all the skills and knowledge you brought to this book—without you it could never have been achieved.

*Peter Fiduccia, August 2012*

Library of Congress Cataloging-in-Publication Data is available on file.

ISBN: 978-1-61608-816-3
Printed in the United States of America

---

## NOTICE TO READERS

This book provides useful instructions, but we cannot anticipate all of your working conditions or the characteristics of your materials and tools. For safety, you should use good judgment, caution, and care when following procedures outlined in this book. Consider your own skill level and the instructions and safety precautions associated with the various tools and materials shown. Neither the publisher nor authors can assume responsibility for any damage to property or injury to persons as a result of misuse of the information provided.

Mid-Continent Public Library
15616 East US Highway 24
Independence, MO 64050

# TABLE OF CONTENTS

# TABLE OF CONTENTS

# SAFETY

In all the projects in this book, especially the tree stands, the designs and methods have been reviewed for safety. We cannot overstate the importance of keeping safety uppermost in your mind when doing the actual work. Safety is the number one priority and should be treated as such. Use the safest construction methods when building any project. Below are what some might consider basic dos and don'ts, but even so they are worth mentioning. These are meant to be safety reminders, but remember that nothing mentioned below replaces good old common sense when it comes to safety.

The one crucial point to remember when using tools is that accidents happen without warning and most important, without much time to react. Your reflexes will not prevent an injury from happening, so stay alert!

• Read the manufacturer's instructions before using any tool, especially if it is your first time at it. Follow all the warnings and cautions. Never force a tool to do anything it was not designed to do.

• When using power tools, always use the safety guards installed on your equipment—they are there for your protection.

• When working in your shop, consider the use of a dust vacuum system to reduce your exposure to airborne sawdust.

• Take your time! Don't rush when undertaking any of the projects in this book. Be cautious, always wear ear, hands, foot, and eye protection. Follow procedures as described in this book and other referenced material and use good judgment.

•    When using electrical power tools and extension cords, make sure the plugs are intact and the wire is not frayed. Don't overload circuits, and always use Ground Fault Circuit Interrupter (GFCI) outlets or cords equipped with GFCI protection. Don't work in wet or damp locations with electrical tools.

•    When creating dust from sawing or sanding, wear a disposable face mask.

•    Always keep your hands away from blades, cutters, bits, and saw teeth.

•    When you are tired, take a break or quit for the day. Completing the project can always wait until tomorrow. Don't work when taking certain medications that might impair your motor skills or judgment.

•    Light up your work area, whether it is outside or indoors.

•    When help is needed, ask for it. Some of these projects need extra sets of hands.

•    To prevent getting caught in rotating equipment or tools, avoid wearing loose clothing or jewelry. Keep long hair tied. Never wear loose clothing when using power tools.

•    Keep the blades and edges of your tools sharp. Avoid using dull tools, since injuries are more likely to occur, and you will also be less satisfied with your results.

•    Neither the authors nor Woods 'N Water Press assumes any responsibility for accidents, injuries, damages, or other possible losses incurred as a direct result of information provided in this book.

# TOOLS AND MATERIALS

## TOOLS

This book takes you through the logistics of creating various archery projects for your lodge, camp, or home, made from wood, plastics, and various other materials. Most of the projects you will be able to build on your own; others will require help from your buddy. When you do need help, don't hesitate to ask for it—pushing yourself and trying to do it all on your own is not safe. The tree stands are clearly projects that you will need help with. You will find each project in every chapter useful, practical, and in many cases fun as well.

It is important to keep in mind the old adage "tools make the job easier" when building any project in this book. Well, I'm not sure that is an old adage, but it is certainly a true one! By using the right tools, you will save yourself time, money, and most of all aggravation. Using quality tools will also help to make each project you build one that you will be proud of. Before you spend a single cent on buying wood to build a project, save your money and make sure you purchase the right tools to do the jobs included in this book. Use old wood, scraps of wood, or wood lying around in the barn before using old and damaged tools. Remember some other things when it comes to tools: Use decent quality tools; use them for what they were intended for; take proper care and maintain them, and these tools will last you a lifetime. My problem is that I can't resist buying the new tools, since the manufacturers are always making improvements and creating more ergonomic tools. I wind up selling my older tools to the newcomers in the trade. Creating the projects in this book can require using a lot of tools, or just a few.

Following are some of the tools needed to make the various projects in this book. You may decide to add to the list or get started with fewer tools (although we don't recommend that). It is our opinion that all the projects will benefit from being built with the kind of quality, technically advanced tools that are available today at very affordable prices. The tools can be broken into two different categories, hand tools and power tools. Power tools can be divided further into portable and stationary power tools.

Many of the projects in this book can be made with just hand tools. After all, how do you think the old-timers built wood projects before the advent of electricity? Obviously, power tools make the job quicker, easier, and in some cases safer as long as the power tools are used with care (see the safety chapter).

We have included a wide range of tools that all do the job required for the projects included. I won't claim to have a favorite brand, since in my opinion each one has its own strengths and weaknesses. The brands of tools vary from the Skil line, to Craftsman, Black & Decker, and Bosch, to name just a few.

Browse through the tools carefully and check out whatever strikes your fancy on the Web sites included. Or you can visit Lowe's or Home Depot, and actually hold each different tool in your hands to see what brand best fits your grip—and your budget, as well. You can also swing a few hammers and hold some other hand tools too, while you're there.

Now take this book down to your shop or workbench, turn to your favorite project, and get started building one of the useful and fun items Leo and I have included just for you!

# HAND TOOLS & POWER TOOLS

## HAMMER

Craftsman 16 oz. Rip Claw Hammer

Sears item #00903821000 Mfr. model #3821

Hammers vary in shape, size, and material such as wood or metal. Use the hammer that fits best in your hand. It can weigh from 16 to 24 ounces. You should be able to drive a nail into wood effortlessly. The claw is used to remove nails.

## TABLE SAW

Bosch 10" Worksite Table Saw with Folding Stand

Model 4000-07

A stationary electric saw can be used to cut wood straight or to make angle cuts. They come in a variety of sizes, but I recommend a 10-inch saw that will cover most of your needs. The wood is pushed along the flat surface toward the blade. This saw is much more precise and accurate than a portable circular saw.

## VARIOUS DRILL BITS

Milwaukee 29-piece Jobbers Twist Drill Bit Kit

Model 48-89-0010

The most common type of drill bit is the twist drill bit, which can be used to drill holes in wood or metal. Since drill bits vary in size, I suggest purchasing a combination kit such as the one shown here. It will cover most of your needs. If a bit breaks, then replace just that one so your kit stays complete.

## HAND SAW

Craftsman 20 in. Hand Saw

Sears item #00936245000 Mfr. model #XP2030-500-SEA

Hand saws come in an endless variety of sizes and shapes. They are sometimes more convenient for smaller jobs, but can be less precise than power saws. A taper ground saw is best for cutting exterior-grade lumber. A ripsaw is best for ripping boards or for cutting trim. A cross-cut saw is best for cutting across the grain. A combination saw does both and is what I recommend.

## RADIAL ARM SAW

Craftsman Professional Laser Trac 10 in. Radial Arm Saw

Sears item #00922010000 Mfr. model #22010

A stationary electric saw can be used to cut wood straight or to make angle cuts. They come in a variety of sizes, but I would recommend a 10-inch saw that will cover most of your needs. This saw differs from the table saw in that the blade rides on a guide and is pulled across to make crosscuts. If used for ripping, the blade guide is rotated 90 degrees and then the wood is pushed toward the blade as with a table saw, except that the blade cuts from above, while a table saw cuts from below.

## ROUTER BIT SET

Skil 91024 24-Piece Carbide Router Bit Set in Wooden Storage Case

Router bits come in a wide variety of sizes and cutting profiles. The 1/4" shank is the most popular. I recommend purchasing a combination kit, which includes most of the bits you will need.

## PVC HAND SAW

Lenox 12" PVC/ABS Hand Saw

PART#: HSF12

This PVC/ABS hand saw's wide, rigid carbon steel blade with hardened teeth will breeze through any diameter plastic pipe, wood, and nail-embedded wood. Its heavy-duty, lightweight aluminum handle features a comfortable hand grip and a large opening for maximum finger clearance, allowing room for work gloves.

## MITER BOX

Companion Miter Box with Saw

Sears item #00936317000 Mfr. model #36317

These come in a variety of sizes and can be made of wood, metal, or plastic. They all help greatly with getting straight cuts and 45-degree angle cuts. I have several wooden miter boxes that are at least 20 years old.

## CORDLESS DRILL

Skil 14.4 Volt Cordless Drill/Driver with Built-In Bit Size Indicator #2567-02

Very popular and extremely versatile, this drill is a must-have in any shop and comes in handy in the field as well. Available in a variety of sizes, cordless drills can be used for drilling holes in wood, with a variety of drill bits. The drill can also be used to drive in screws and extract them by attaching different screwdriver tips.

## HOLE SAW SET

Bosch Power Change Bi-metal Hole Saw Master set, 11 pc. Model PC11PCM

Hole saws are used with a drill to cut a set size hole in wood. They vary in size from 3/8-inch up to 5 inches. A combination kit will provide you with the most common sizes needed for the projects in this book.

## SCREWDRIVERS

Craftsman12-piece Screwdriver Set, Powerhouse

Sears item #00941619000 Mfr. model #41619

The types, sizes, and shapes are endless. I suggest buying a standard combination set, which should meet most demands.

## POWER DRILL
Craftsman 9-26946 6 amp 3/8" Drive Corded Drill, Variable Speed Keyless Chuck DANTOO 9-26946

Similar to the cordless drill, except it can only be used in the shop and in the field as unless you have access to power. It can be used with a variety of bits for drilling holes in wood of any thickness. The advantage of this over the cordless drill is that you don't have to worry about the battery depleting and having to recharge it.

## CHISEL
Craftsman 3-piece Wood Chisel Set

Sears item #00936857000 Mfr. model #36857

Chisels come in a variety of shapes and sizes. I recommend buying a combination set ranging in size from 1/4 inch to 1 inch that will handle most jobs.

## ROUTER
Craftsman 9-26834 Professional 2 hp 9.5 amp Router with Carrying Bag DANTOO 9-26834

Used with a variety of bits, which extend past the bottom surface used to smooth, hollow out, or decorate wood edges.

## CARPENTER'S SQUARE
Companion 8 x 12-inch Carpenter's Square

Sears item #00939654000 Mfr. model #39654

Also known as a speed square. This is a triangular square that is used to measure and check 45-degree and 90-degree angles.

## PALM SANDER
Craftsman6-inch Palm Sander

Sears item #00919960000 Mfr. model #19960

A handheld electric sander, which works with all grades of sand paper, makes sanding of large or small surfaces much easier.

## COMBINATION SQUARE

Empire 6-inch Pocket Combination Square

Sears item #00939271000 Mfr. model #255N

This square is used for measuring 45-degree and 90-degree angles. It also can be used as a depth gauge and a ruler.

## BELT SANDER

Craftsman 9-11726 8.0-amp Belt Sander DANTOO 9-11726

A handheld electric sander works with all grades of sandpaper and is used to make sanding of large surfaces much easier. As opposed to the palm sander, this sander is used for the bigger projects and care must be taken to avoid digging into the wood, as the belt sandpaper tends to be more aggressive.

## TORPEDO LEVEL

Craftsman Solid Aluminum Torpedo Level

Sears item #00939819000 Mfr. model #991-10

This little device comes in handy when you want to make sure that the object is level, either vertically or horizontally.

## JIGSAW/SABER SAW

Bosch 24V Cordless Jigsaw Kit Model #52324

This saw is excellent for making curved cuts, straight cuts, and angle cuts. It is used to cut out holes for windows, doors, or round shapes. A variety of blades can be used, depending on the wood you are cutting and the finish you want. Cord and cordless models are available.

## RATCHET SET

Craftsman 12-piece Socket Wrench Set, SAE

Sears item #00934745000 Mfr. model #34745

The types and sizes are endless. I recommend a standard combination set that will meet most of your needs. If you use metric bolts, nuts, and screws, buy a metric combination set.

## SCREW GUN

Craftsman Companion 4.8 volt Pistol Screwdriver

Sears item #00910175000 Mfr. model #10175

Used solely for putting screws in place and removing them. Although hand screwdrivers can be used, this battery-powered one with the correct bit makes the job much easier.

## WRENCHES

Craftsman 8-piece Ratcheting Wrench Set, SAE

Sears item #00942444000 Mfr. model #42444

Here again, the types and sizes are endless. I recommend a standard combination set that will meet most of your needs. If you use metric bolts, nuts, and screws, buy a metric combination set.

## CHAIN SAW

Craftsman 18-inch Gas Chain Saw

Sears item #07135082000 Mfr. model #358350820

These come in various sizes as specified by the chain length. Don't bother with electric chain saws—go for the gas-powered saws, which are much more versatile. The 18-inch size will cover most jobs.

## STAPLE GUN

Arrow Fastener Professional Staple & Nail Gun

Sears item #00974486000 Mfr. model #T50P9N

A staple gun comes in handy for stapling cloth, thin wood, or wire mesh.

## AIR-POWERED NAIL GUN

Home Depot - Paslode 16-Gauge Cordless Straight Finish Nailer

Model 902000

These come in a variety of sizes and brands, with the air power provided by an air compressor, or cartridges for the portable types. They tend be expensive, but once you use one, you will never want to hand-nail again. For starters, I suggest buying the portable one, as it will come in handy for most of the projects in this book, particularly the tree stands. A variety of nail sizes can be used, depending on the type of gun used.

## POWER MITER BOX
Makita LS1013 10-inch Slide Dual Compound Miter Saw MAKUSA LS1013

This is a stationary saw used to make straight wood cuts or angle cuts. Once you've tried one, you will never want to use a hand miter box again. The wood is placed on the bottom surface and held in place, and the blade is brought down on the wood to make the cut.

## SHOVEL
Companion Long Handle Round Point Fiberglass Shovel

Sears item #07183830000 Mfr. model #45011

We all know what shovels are used for. This one will cover all your digging needs.

## CIRCULAR SAW

Craftsman 9-10860 14.0-amp 7 1/4-inch Circular Saw with Laser-Trac™ and Case DANTOO 9-10860

This is probably the most important portable electric tool for fast and accurate cuts. It can be used for just about every project in this book. When making long straight cuts it is suggested to use a straightedge guide. They come in a variety of sizes, with the 7 1/4–inch blade size, which is the most popular, and will handle most cuts.

## TAPE MEASURE
Craftsman 1-inch x 30 ft. Steel Tape Measure

Sears item #00939676000 Mfr. model #39676

This in one tool you can't do without. They come in a variety of sizes and lengths. The 30-foot tape will cover all jobs in this book.

# WOOD FILE
Craftsman 10-inch Smooth Shoe Rasp

Sears item #00931286000 Mfr. model #31286

A metal file used for smoothing and shaping wood.

# WOOD PLANE
Footprint Tools Block Plane, 7 x 1 5/8 inches

Sears item #00937740000 Mfr. model #4B

A tool used to smooth and straighten the surface of a piece of wood. The plane should cut in the direction of the wood grain.

# HAND PRUNING SAW
Craftsman 10-inch Folding Pruning Saw

Sears item #07185302000 Mfr. model #79476968

Used to cut or prune tree limbs. These saws are not as fine-toothed as a hand saw is. A folding handle is nice feature if you intend on carrying it in your pocket.

# POLE SAW
Pump N' Cut Ropeless Tree Pruner

Sears item #07186393000 Mfr. model #92366941

Similar to a pruning saw, only the blade is attached to a long extendable pole enabling you to reach up high into the tree limbs. A must-have when placing tree stands.

# NAIL SET
Craftsman 3-piece Nail Set

Sears item #00937354000 Mfr. model #781

Nails sets, which come in a variety of sizes, are used to set the head of a finish nail below the surface of the wood. This combination set is a good way to go.

## WOOD CLAMPS

Jorgensen 18-inch Steel Bar Clamp

Sears item #00931744000 Mfr. model #3718-HD

These come in handy when you need to temporarily secure wood or hold it down on a table perfectly still while sawing, drilling, or sanding.

## RAKE

Used to grade the ground prior to setting your shed.

## POST HOLE DIGGER—HAND

SEYMOUR-DG60 Promotional Post Hole Digger

Used to dig holes in dirt for installing posts.

## UTILITY KNIFE

Bostitch Interlock Self-Retracting Utility Knife BOS 10189C

Used to cut vinyl or plastic material and cardboard. The spring-loaded blade retracts into this utility knife automatically when pressure on the slide button is released. Round point blade reduces risk of accidental cuts and damage to the interior contents of cartons.

# MATERIALS

The materials used in making the majority of the projects in this book include wood, plastics such as PVC, antler sheds, fasteners, and finishing materials. Each project description lists the sizes and types of wood, along with the types of fasteners suggested to be used. The finishing material is suggested but can be varied depending upon your preferences.

The wood used depends upon whether the project is intended for outdoor or indoor use. If it is to be exposed to the weather, the wood used should be durable, long-lasting, and resistant to moisture and insects. If the project is intended for indoor use, then the choice of wood is yours. We have suggested the best types of wood to use based upon how our projects have been constructed.

The most commonly used exterior woods for these projects include exterior-grade lumber such as alkaline copper quaternary (ACQ) and cedar. Other woods are available, such as redwood and mahogany, but these are much more expensive. We went with the more affordable woods for most projects. ACQ-treated lumber is now the wood of choice for outdoor construction, and has replaced lumber treated with chromated copper arsenate (CCA). Cedar is fairly lightweight and is very easy to work with. Our preferred woods for interior projects or interior surfaces include pine, Douglas fir, oak, and poplar. Pine is still relatively inexpensive, easy to work with, and finishes nicely either with a stain or clear finish. Douglas fir is used for interior framing and is also easy to work with.

Oak is a member of the hardwood family, a bit more difficult to work with, a bit more expensive, but worth it when you are looking for a richer-looking finished project. It finishes very nicely with either a clear finish or a stain. If you are going to paint the project, poplar is a good choice. It is a relatively hard wood and takes a painted finish (use a few coats) nicely.

The lumber dimensions are also given for each project. The actual size of the lumber is given, as opposed to the nominal dimension of standard lumber. For example, a nominal 1x6 actually measures at 3/5 x 5 1/2"; a 2x4 measures at 1 1/2 x 3 1/2"; a 2x10 measure at 1 1/2 x 9 1/4" and so on.

The fasteners used for these projects are listed in each chapter. For the most part, they include nails and screws. For interior use, nails or screws do not have to be corrosion-resistant, and common or bright nails and uncoated screws will work fine. For exterior use, nails and screws need to be coated with a protective coating, or made of brass or stainless steel. These tend be more expensive, so we made use of coated fasteners. The most common coatings are galvanized, anodized, and zinc plated. Galvanized steel is the least expensive and most common. When using ACQ lumber, don't use galvanized nails or screws, because the ACQ coating will cause galvanized fasteners to corrode. There are a variety of fastener coatings suitable for use with ACQ, so check with your supplier to make sure you get the proper type.

The finishes used will depend on your taste and where your project will be placed and how it will blend with your existing decor. Some woods, such as cedar and oak, will look really nice with clear finishes such as transparent stain or varnishes and shellacs. They can also be stained to any desired color or shade, left unfinished, or coated with a clear finish once stained. Paint can also be used, and we recommend latex-based paint. Any finish used outdoors must be a weatherproof, exterior-grade paint, stain, or clear finish.

# 1

# ARROWHEAD GAME PLAQUE

## TOOLS

Drill and 1/2" hole saw, 3/8" drill bit

Router with 45-degree bit

Circular saw

Jigsaw

Small triangular file

Palm sander or belt sander

As an avid bowhunter and gun hunter as well, I have recently started a new tradition. For any trophy buck I decide to mount, I not only make my own plaque to save some money, but those taken with a bow have plaques made to remind me how the game was taken—not that I could forget the details of any of my hunts!

This project is fairly simple to make, using a piece of oak ply-wood. Any other plywood can be used, such a birch, redwood, or cherry. It is cut in the shape of a broadhead, with the edges beveled using a router and painted black to represent the edge of an arrowhead. The plaque is stained with a Provincial (soft brown) stain. Two 3-inch-long Shaker pegs are mounted at the bottom of the plaque to display the arrow used to harvest the trophy. The plaque can be made smaller or larger depending on the size of the trophy. Simply modify the shape of the pattern accordingly to ensure that the widest part of the head fits nicely within the plaque.

Other woods can be used, including less expensive softwoods such as pine. However, you may have to glue several planks together, since most standard boards are no wider than 16 inches, adding to the complexity of this project. Another problem with the softwoods is that they will dent easily, but that can be resolved by using a good coat of stain and shellac.

The type of wood and finish you choose can be determined by your budget and personal preference. We prefer hardwoods because they look richer when finished and the wood grain stands out more. No matter what you use, however, you will feel a deep sense of satisfaction in making your own deer mounting plaque as well as saving money.

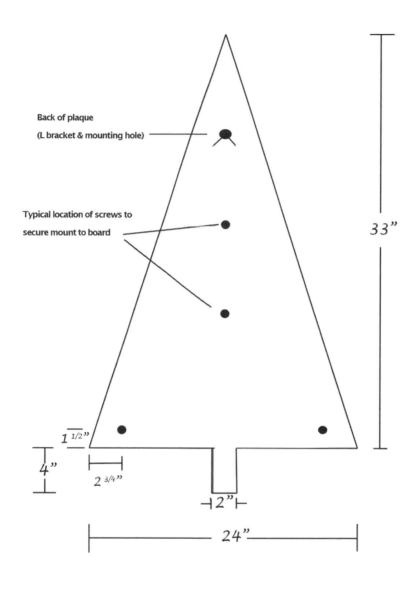

Figure 1

Dimensions: 37 inches high, 24 inches wide

## CUTTING LIST

| Key | Part | Dimensions | Pcs. | Material |
|-----|------|-----------|------|----------|
| A | Plaque | 3/4 x 25 x 40" | 1 | Oak plywood |

**Materials:** 3"x 3" flat L bracket, 10 d nail or heavy-duty picture frame hook (rated at 50 pounds or more); finish-stain, varnish, and black paint; two 3/8" x 3" long Shaker pegs.

**Note:** Measurements reflect the actual thickness of dimension lumber.

**Directions:** Cut and shape the wall plaque as shown in Figure 1.

1. Cut the overall dimension of the plaque.

2. Using the pattern shown in Figure 1, draw the actual shape onto the plaque.

3. Cut the outline using a circular saw. In order to get a straight cut, clamp a guide board along the measured line. A jigsaw can be used to cut the bottom shaft end if desired.

4. Sand the edge using a belt sander or palm sander.

5. Shape the entire edge of the plaque using a router with a 1/2" 45-degree bit. Turn the board over and repeat for the edge on the opposite side. This will make the edge look like a razor-sharp arrowhead.

6. Sand off the routered edge. If there are any imperfections on the routered edge, use wood putty to fill them in before sanding smooth.

7. Using a triangular small file, score the outside 45-degree front edge. Make the scores every 1/2" around the entire edge. This gives the appearance of a serrated edge.

## Make the rear mounting bracket.

1. Drill a 1/2" hole approximately 3/8" deep into the back of the plaque (about 9" below the top center of the plaque). Take care not to drill through the plaque's front face.

2. Install a 2x2 flat L bracket with 3/8" wood screws. Place the bracket so that the inside corner just covers the top of the hole

Here is how using a guide board clamped along the measuring line will help you keep a straight edge when cutting with a circular saw. The straight edge above is a 1" x 3" strip of poplar.

drilled in the plywood. This type of hanging bracket is recommended if the deer head is larger and heavier than normal.

## APPLY FINISHING TOUCHES

1. Sand the entire surface and edges using the palm sander or belt sander.

2. Drill two 3/8" holes for the pegs 5/8" deep, in the locations shown in Figure 1.

3. Use a dab of wood glue at the end of each peg and insert into the holes, allow time to dry.

4. Paint the edge with black enamel paint. Apply at least two coats. Sand between coats.

5. Apply the desired color stain to the front surface of the plaque. Recoat to desired shade. Apply varnish or wax finish as desired.

Secure the deer head mount to the plaque and hang the completed plaque to the wall.

1. Drill at least two holes through the back of the plaque along the centerline. Use two wood screws, and secure to the back of the deer head. Make sure that the deer head is placed evenly within the plaque.

2. The plaque can be mounted anywhere on a wall, prefer-ably along a stud. When you decide where to install the plaque, locate the 2x4 studs in the wall. They should be about 16" apart on center.

3. Place the plaque on the wall and mark the corresponding stud location onto the back support. Use a 10 d nail or a large-headed wood screw and secure to a stud so that no more than 1/2" of the head is protruding past the wall surface. A heavy-duty picture frame hook (rated at least 50 pounds) can be used instead of a nail.

4. Mount the plaque so that the nail, screw head, or frame hook rests in the back of the L bracket.

**Tip:** This plaque can be made smaller or larger to accommodate the head size of your elk or deer. To resize, simply adjust the pattern accordingly.

# 2

# ARCHER'S PICTURE FRAME

This DIY project is one you can enjoy in your home or your weekend cabin.

---

### TOOLS

Hand saw and miter box or power miter box

Hammer

Router

2 flute straight plunge bit, 20mm diameter, 1/4" shank

2 flute round over bit, 3/8" radius, 1/4" shank

2 flute rabbeting bit, 3/8" depth, 1/4" shank

---

It wasn't long after we purchased our second piece of property, which is part of our family hunting camp, that the call for this project was made. We named one area of this 110-acre tract Middle Earth. It's an area where we have jumped a nice buck several times over the past few seasons, and we have finally concluded that the best time to get this buck is during the bow season. The canvas painting was done by a close friend. The painting shows Middle Earth on our property. The trail, which is approximately 500 yards long, connects our front field with the upper field. Several tree stands have been strategically placed on both sides of the trail in anticipation of this fall bowhunting season. Only time will tell.

This frame was built to hold an oil painting in a matte that measures 18" x 24," which is a standard size. It's a simple matter to adjust the measurements if your oil painting is smaller or larger. If the frame is made smaller, I would suggest adjusting the width of the actual frame pieces from 2 1/2" to 2" or smaller. Obviously, you can substitute your favorite wildlife print or portrait for the oil painting.

We used clear pine for this project. It was stained with a light Provincial stain and finished with a clear coat of polyurethane. Other woods can be used, such as oak, cherry, or cedar if you want a different look. The woods can easily be stained and then finished with a clear coat to match the decor of your room.

Building this frame will help save you money for purchasing other paintings or wildlife prints. Instead of having to buy them already framed, you can buy them unframed and save at least 50 to 75 percent off the retail cost! The savings realized by building your own frames will allow you to purchase more paintings. The materials you need to buy to build this frame won't break the bank, either.

This is one of our favorite projects because of its simplicity to build, the handsomeness it adds to any space, and the savings it provides. It also gets the most compliments from everyone who sees it. Build this frame as one of your first projects, and the satisfaction you will get from this will motivate you to move on to other projects in this book!

Dimensions: 28 3/8" wide, 22 3/8" long

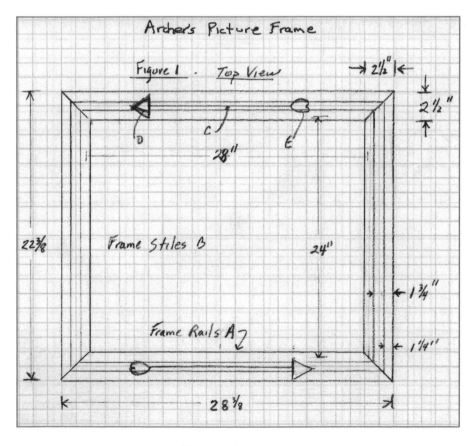

Figure 1 - Top View

9

## CUTTING LIST

| Key | Part | Dimensions | Pcs. | Material |
|-----|------|-----------|------|----------|
| A | Frame rails | 3/4" x 2 1/2" x 28 3/8 | 2 | Pine |
| B | Frame stiles | 3/4" x 2 1/2" x 22 3/8 | 2 | Pine |
| C | Arrow shafts | 1/4" x 15" | 2 | Birch |
| D | Arrow heads | 1/4" x 2 1/2" x 24" | 2 | Birch |
| E | Arrow vanes | 3/16" x 2 3/4" x 1 3/8 | 2 | Birch |
| F | Backing | 1/8" x 18" x 24" | 1 | Luan |

**Materials:** Wood glue; 3/8" corrugated joint fasteners; polyurethane, lacquer, and/or stain; 1/8" glass or Plexiglas 24" x 18"; framer's points; picture frame wire and eyelets.

Note: Measurements reflect the actual thickness of dimension lumber. The arrow heads and the arrow vanes can be made from 1/4"stock, or more simply, purchased at an arts and crafts store. They are also available at www.craftparts.com.

**Directions:** Measure and cut all the pieces (A), (B), (C), and (F) as shown in cutting list. Use a hand saw and miter box or power miter box to get the 45 degree cuts at the ends of the rails and stiles.

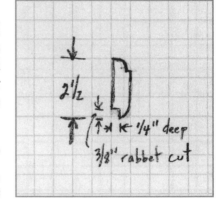

Figure 2

1. Using a router with a 3/8" rabbeting bit set at a depth of 1/4", cut along the back sides on the inside edges of the rails (A) and stiles (B). This will provide the setback for the glass, photo, and backing.

2. Using a straight plunge bit, 20mm diameter, set at a depth of 1/4", make the straight cuts on the front surfaces of the rails (A) and stiles (B). Set the router guide from the outside edges, as shown in Figure 1.

3. Using a router with a 3/8" round over bit run it over the outside edges of the rails (A) and stiles (B). Set the depth of the router bit to duplicate the shape, as shown in Figure 2.

4. Using the same router with a 3/8" round over bit run it over the inside edges of the rails (A) and stiles (B). Lower the depth of the router bit to duplicate the shape, as shown in Figure 2.

5. Lay out the two frame stiles (B) on the front side against a flat work surface about 28 1/2" apart.

6. Lay the frame rails (A) between the two frame stiles (B), as shown in Figure 1.

7. Put a dab of wood glue at the four surfaces where the stiles meet the rails.

8. Make sure your frame corners are square using a square or by measuring the frame's diagonals (from corner to corner). When the frame is square the diagonals are equal.

9. Use wood clamps on the top and bottom of each stile and tighten them so that the stiles are snug against the rails. Using a hammer, nail two 3/8" corrugated joint fastener in each corner ensuring that the joint is tight, as shown in Figure 3.

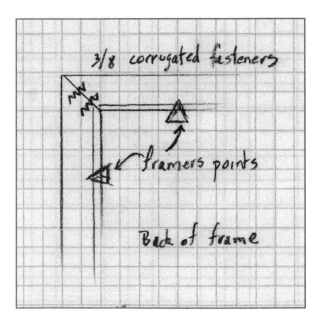

Figure 3

Check again for square and allow the glue to dry for several hours.

10. When the glue is dry, remove the clamps.

11. Sand smooth all surfaces using 120-grain sandpaper.

## APPLY FINISHING TOUCHES

1. Turn the frame over and place the front on a flat surface.

2. Using wood glue, attach an arrow shaft on the front surface of the top rail, centered between the two straight cuts and centered within the rail length.

3. Using wood glue, attach an arrowhead (D) on one end of the shaft.

4. If the arrow vane-shaped pieces (E) were purchased at an arts and crafts store or online, cut approximately 1/4" off the triangular end. Using wood glue, attach an arrow vane (E) on the other end of the shaft.

5. Repeat Steps 2–4 for the bottom rail.

6. Apply the finish of your choice.

7. Place the glass or Plexiglas inside the frame opening.

8. Lay your favorite print or picture inside the frame on top of the glass.

9. Place the backing (F) on top of the print.

10. Secure it in place by using a small hammer to drive four or five framer's points into the sides of the rails and stiles. Make sure that they are pressing against the backing.

11. Secure the eyelets on the backside of the frame for the hanging wire, about 5 inches down from the top of the frame on each side of the stiles.

12. Twist the wire into each of the eyelets so that there is about an inch of slack in the wire.

13. Hang the frame on a wall in your favorite location.

Author's note: If you use a picture that was painted on a canvas back board, you won't need to use the backing as described above. Simply lay the portrait on top of the glass or Plexiglas and mount in the same manner as described above.

# 3

# ARCHERY WORKBENCH

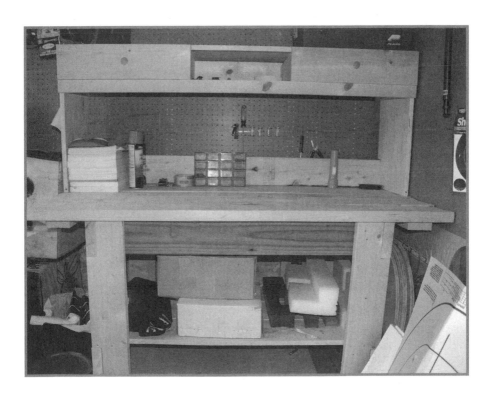

## TOOLS

Hand saw or circular saw

Table saw

Tape measure

T-square or combination square

Hammer

Drill and 1/8" bit

Screw gun

As we mentioned in our previous book, 25 *Projects for Outdoorsmen,* once you build a bench like this you will want more—they are extremely handy. So we made some modifications and came up with this design.

This bench is made of two sections, the lower bench and the upper shelf and drawer section. The bottom section has a lower shelf to store tools and other archery equipment. The upper section also has a pegboard, a handy place to hang your archery work tools and accessories.

The project calls for using relatively inexpensive lumber such as Douglas fir. It is a very easy project to make and put together and is solid enough to tackle the kinds of jobs that more elaborate and expensive work benches are known for. Although it's not included with this bench, a vise can easily be mounted along the front edge.

The drawings show typical dimensions. Instructions are given below and it's easy enough to adjust the size of the bench to better match your body height, available wall space, and the type of viseyou will need for the type of work you will be doing on the bench. The pegboard behind the bench is great for hanging tools, accessories, and miscellaneous items. The actual hooks come in a variety of designs depending on what tool you need to hang. We used heavy 1/4-inch pegboard. It's easier to put up and it will not "give" when you hang or remove tools.

Dimensions: 83" high; 60" long; 30" wide

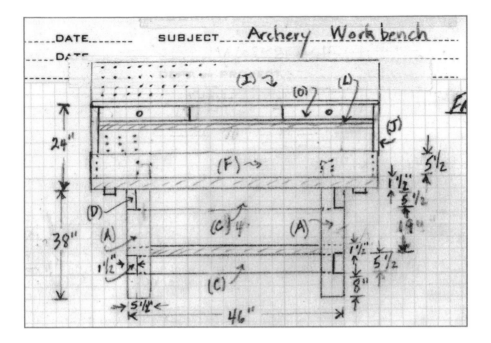

Figure 1 - Front View

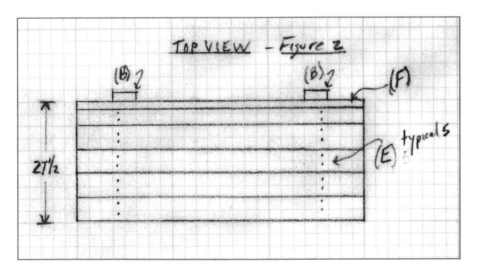

Figure 2 - Top View

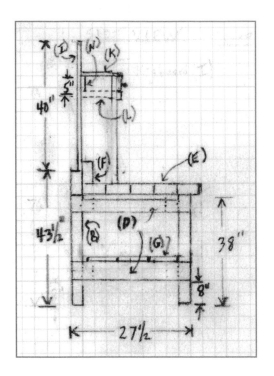

Figure 3
Slide View

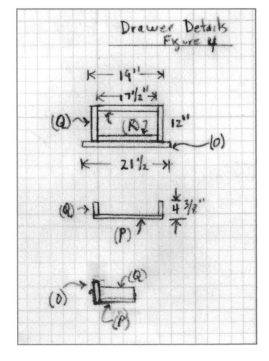

Figure 4
Drawer Details

# CUTTING LIST

| Key | Part | Dimensions | Pcs. | Material |
|-----|------|------------|------|----------|
| A | Front legs | 1 1/2" x 5 1/2" x 38" | 2 | Douglas fir |
| B | Rear legs | 1 1/2" x 5 1/2" x 43 1/2" | 2 | Douglas fir |
| C | Front/rear leg supports | 1 1/2" x 5 1/2" x 40" | 4 | Douglas fir |
| D | Side leg supports | 1 1/2" x 5 1/2" x 27 1/2" | 4 | Douglas fir |
| E | Bench top | 1 1/2" x 5 1/2" x 60" | 5 | Douglas fir |
| F | Bench top back | 1 1/2" x 5 1/2" x 60" | 1 | Douglas fir |
| G | Bottom shelf | 3/4" x 7 1/2" x 43" | 3 | Douglas fir |
| H | Bench top braces | 1 1/2" x 2 1/2" x 27 1/2" | 2 | Douglas fir |
| I | Top Pegboard | 1/4" x 60" x 40" | 1 | Masonite |
| J | Drawer sides | 3/4"x 12" x 24" | 2 | Pine |
| K | Drawer Shelf top | 3/4" x 12" x 60" | 1 | Pine |
| L | Drawer Shelf bottom | 3/4" x 12" x 58 1/2" | 1 | Pine |
| M | Drawer spacers | 3/4" x 5" x 11 1/4" | 2 | Pine |
| N | Drawer back | 3/4" x 5" x 57 1/2" | 1 | Pine |
| O | Draw front face | 3/4" x 5 1/2" x 21 1/2" | 2 | Pine |
| P | Draw bottoms | 1/8" x 11 1/4" x 19" | 2 | Pine |
| Q | Draw sides | 3/4" x 4 1/2" x 11 1/4" | 4 | Pine |
| R | Drawer back/front | 3/4" x 4 1/2" x 17 1/2" | 4 | Pine |
| S | Drawer trim | 3/4" x 2" x 60" | 1 | Pine |

**Materials:** Common nails in sizes 10d, 8d, 6d, and 4d, and 1" brads; wood glue; 1 1/4" drywall screws; two 1" wooden knobs.

Note: Measurements reflect the actual thickness of dimension lumber.

**Directions:**

**Construct the bench base.**

1. Measure and cut pieces (A), (B), (C), and (D) as shown incutting list. Use a hand saw or circular saw.

2. Notch out the front legs (A) and rear legs (B) as follows. From the bottom of the legs, measure 8" up and 5 1/2" and square off marks 1 1/2" deep. Measure from that point 19" up and 5 1/2" and square off marks 1 1/2" deep. Using a hand saw, (or a circular or table saw if available) make 1 1/2" cuts into the legs at the marks. Using a hand chisel, notch out the 5 1/2" blocks. Refer to Figure 1, front view.

Note: The rear legs (B) are 5 inches longer than the front legs (A) to provide support for mounting the bench top back (F) in the next section.

3. Lay out one of the front legs (A) and rear legs (B) approximately 28" apart on your work surface. Use two side leg supports (D), and place them in the notched-out cuts. Make sure that the ends of the side supports are flush with the fronts and backs of the legs. Using wood glue and 10d nails, nail the side leg supports into the legs with three nails at each location. Use the T-square to ensure that all joints are square prior to nailing.

4. Repeat Step 3 for the other side.

5. Set up each of the side leg structures (from Steps 3 and 4) approximately 43" apart in the vertical position. Use two of the front and rear leg supports, and place them in the front notches. Make sure that the ends are snug against the side leg supports. Using wood glue and 8d nails, secure in place by driving three nails into the front legs. Repeat in three other locations. Use two 10d nails, and nail through the side supports into the ends of the front leg supports. Repeat in two other locations.

6. Repeat Step 5 for the rear of the legs.

7. Your bench is now ready for the installation of the top-bench surface and bottom shelf.

**Construct the bench top and shelf.** (See Figures 2 and 3)

1. Measure and cut pieces (E), (F), (G), and (H) as shown in the cutting list, using a hand saw or circular saw.

2. Place the five bench top (E) pieces on top of the bench base. Make sure that the bench top overhangs evenly on both ends, by approximately 7". Using wood glue and 10d nails, secure the top inplace by nailing through the top into the top side leg supports (D). Use two nails in each location, and make sure that the bench top-pieces are snug against each other.

3. Place the bench top back (F) on top of the bench top, against the rear leg supports. Using wood glue and 8d nails, secure in place by nailing from the bottom side of the rear top bench piece into the end of the top back. Drive two 8d nails into the rear support.

4. Position each of the bench top braces (H) underneath the top bench. Secure in place by using wood glue and 6d nails, nailing into the bench top. Position these braces evenly on both sides.

5. Place the bottom shelf (G) pieces on the lower side leg supports. Space them out evenly between the legs. Using wood glue and 6d nails, secure in place by nailing into the side leg supports.

**Construct the drawer top assembly.** (See Figures 3 and 4)

1. Measure and cut pieces (J), (K), (L), (M), (N), (O), (P), (Q), (R), and (S) as shown in the cutting list. Use a circular saw or table saw.

2. Lay out the drawer sides (J) on a flat surface approximately 60" apart.

3. Place the drawer shelf top (K) on top of the sides. Secure in place by using wood glue and three 6d nails along the edge.

4. Place the drawer shelf bottom (L) between the shelf sides (J) at the locations shown in Figure 3. Secure in place by using wood glue and three 6d nails at each location.

5. Notch out the bottoms of both sides. Measure 1 1/2" and 5" from the bottom rear of the side. Using a hand saw, cut the notch. This will allow you to fit the top assembly against the bench top back (F).

6. Place the drawer back (N) between the drawer shelf top (K) and bottom (L) in the rear of the drawer top assembly. Secure in place using wood glue and six 6d nails along the top and bottom edges.

7. Position the two drawer spacers (M) between the drawer shelf top (K) and bottom (L) at 19 1/8" from each side. Secure in place by driving three 6d nails from the top and the bottom.

8. Place the drawer trim (S) on the face of the drawer shelf bottom (L) so it is flush with the top edge of the shelf. Secure in place using wood glue and six 6d nails.

9. Assemble the drawers. Secure the drawer sides (Q) to the drawer rears and fronts, using wood glue and two 8d nails in each end. Secure the drawer bottom (P) to the bottom of the drawer assembly using wood glue and 1" brads along all four edges. Repeat for the other drawer.

10. Mount the drawer front face (O) to the drawer assembly. Make sure that it overhangs both ends evenly and the bottom edge lies flush with the bottom of the drawer. Secure in place by using wood glue and 10 4d nails from the inside of the drawer assembly.

11. Drill an 1/8" hole in the center of both drawer front faces and mount the wooden knobs.

12. Place the completed drawer assembly into the slots oneach side.

## Secure the pegboard, drawer top assembly, and bench in place.

1. Position the drawer assembly on top of the bench top so that the sides are flush with the ends of the bench top and against the bench top back (F).

2. Place the top pegboard (I) in place on top of the bench top back (F). Screw into place by using 1 1/4" drywall screws. Use six screws along the bottom into (F). Use another six screws into the back of (N). Use two screws along each end into the rear edge of (J).

3.  The bench can be left free standing or secured in place against a wall. I highly recommend it be secured to a wall if a vise is mounted to the bench top. Use two 4" x 3/8" lag bolts with washers on each rear leg, and drill 3/8" holes through the legs. Secure to the wall studs. For concrete walls, use anchors and secure the lag screws into them.

# 4

# GAME POLE WITH ROOF

**TOOLS**

Hand saw and circular saw

Level

Tape measure

T-square or combination square

Hammer

Staple gun and staples

Screwdriver

Drill and 1/4" drill bit, 3/8" bit 12" long

Post hole digger

Shovel

Rake

Chain saw

This game pole not only provides an elevated post to keep your game off the ground, but also keeps it protected from the sun, rain, and snow. During the off season, we use it as a storage location for one of our tractors.

The overall dimensions can vary depending upon the size of your amp and how successful everyone is. This design can hold up to six average-sized whitetails.

This project was built to last a lifetime. The center posts and center top beam are 8x8 pressure-treated wood. Using a beam like this eliminates any worry about the beam sagging. The outside corner posts and roof supports are 6x6 pressure-treated lumber—sturdy enough to hold any roof load, even in areas where heavy snow is experienced. The overhead roof was finished using standard roofing shingles. If cost is a concern, use rolled roof paper instead. Since we built this close to the house, we wanted the roof to match.

To make things simpler, eliminate the roof and the four corner posts, and follow the appropriate steps to erect the center posts and top center rail. Instead of using the square posts, telephone poles can be used as a substitute.

Dimensions: 12' high; 12' long; 8' wide

## CUTTING LIST

| Key | Part | Dimensions | Pcs. | Material |
|---|---|---|---|---|
| A | Center posts | 7 1/2" x 7 1/2" x 14' | 2 | Pressure-treated ACQ |
| B | Top center rail | 7 1/2" x 7 1/2" x 12' | 1 | Pressure-treated ACQ |
| C | Corner posts | 5 1/2" x 5 1/2" x 14' | 4 | Pressure-treated ACQ |
| D | Top corner rails | 5 1/2" x 5 1/2" x 12' | 2 | Pressure-treated ACQ |
| E | Roof rafters | 2 1/2" x 3 1/2' x 6' | 14 | Pressure-treated ACQ |
| F | Roof | 5/8" x 4' x 8' | 5 | Exterior-grade plywood |
| G | Temporary braces | 2 1/2" x 3 1/2" x 8' | 12 | Douglas fir |

**Materials:** Hot-dipped galvanized nails: 16d, 10d, 8d, 6d, plus 1 1/4" and 1/2" roofing nails; asphalt roofing shingles; 15# rolled asphalt paper, staples; 48' brown metal roof edging; four 8" Tee plates, four 8" L brackets, eight 6" T-plates, 28 TE-CO clamps, five 3/8" x 12" eyebolts with 3/8" washers and nuts; 12 80-pound bags of ready-mix Sakrete mix.

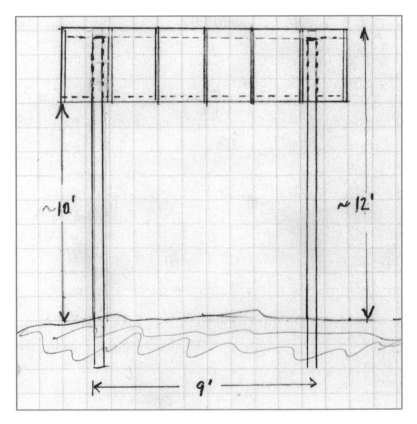

Figure 1

Note: Measurements reflect the actual thickness of dimension lumber.

## Directions:

### Lay out locations of post holes and set in place.

1.  Select the location of the game pole. We placed ours behind our hunting lodge against the backside of the hemlocks, where the ground was relatively flat.

25

2. It is important to get the four outside corner posts square to each other. Lay out one piece of 4 x 8 plywood on the ground; lay another piece along the 4-foot end. Ensure that the plywood pieces are square to each other. Use the outside corner of the plywood, and mark this as the first corner. Measure 9 feet along the plywood and mark this as the next corner post. Now measure 6 feet from the first corner post location, and mark this as the third corner. Measure 9 feet from this corner and mark the location of the fourth corner post.

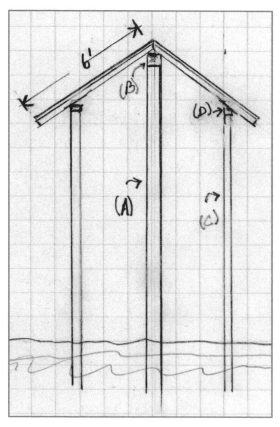

Figure 2
Post Location

3. Using a post hole digger, dig holes at least 36 to 40" deep. This will result in a post height from grade of approximately 10 or 11'.

4. Place a corner post (C) in one of the holes. Mix two bags of ready-mix concrete and pour in the hole. Have someone hold the pole upright. Using a level, make sure the post is plumb and provide temporary braces (G) on two sides of the post. Nail one end of the brace to the post and jam the other end into the dirt. Repeat this step for the other three cornerposts.

5. Measure the middle between the two corner posts and mark the location of the center post (A). Dig a hole at least 24 to 30" deep at this location, and repeat for the other side. This will result in a post height from grade of approximately 11 1/2' to 12'. Follow the same procedure as in Step 4 above, using concrete and temporary braces to secure them in place.

Note: Plan on installing the posts the first day, and allow the concrete to set overnight before proceeding with the remainder of the project.

1. Place the top center rail (B) across the center posts (A). Place a level on top of the rail and check for level. If the tops of the posts are not level, mark the difference, which needs to be cut off the taller post. Remove the rail and using a chain saw, cut the post to the desired height. Place the rail back in place on top of the post. The post should overhang each end by 18". Secure in place by using two 8" L-brackets on each post. Also install two 8" T-plates on each post. Foradded strength, toenail 16d nails in each post-to-rail joint.

2. The four corner posts (C) should be leveled in the same manner as described in Step 6, and the posts should be cut 24" shorter than the height of the center posts. Place the top corner rail (D) on top of two of the corner posts (C) and make sure it overhangs each end by 18". Secure in place by using two 6" T-plates on each post. Foradded strength, toenail 16d nails in each post-to-rail joint. Repeat forthe other side.

3. Fill in the post holes with any leftover dirt and make grade flush.

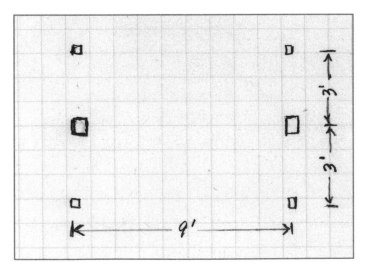

Figure 3

## Frame and sheath roof.

1. Mark out the locations of the roof rafters along the top center rail (B) and both sides of the top corner rails (D) at 24" centers using a square. You will need a helper for the following steps.

2. Starting at either end, place a roof rafter (E) on both sides of the center rail and let them rest on the corner rails. Using a level, mark a line on each end of the rafters where they rest upon the center rail.

3. Using a hand saw or circular saw, cut the end of each rafter.

4. Using one of these as your pattern, mark the same cuts onthe remaining rafters and cut the ends.

5. Starting on either end, lay a rafter on each side of the center rail, butt them together, and toenail into the top center rail using 8d nails. Nail the ends together using a 10d nail. Toenail the rafter into each corner top rail using 8d nails. Using 6d nails, attach a TECO clamp at both joints along the top center rail and on each joint of the top corner rails.

6. Install the remaining six sets of rafters at 24" centers along the rails in the same manner as in Step 5.

7. Install the plywood on the roof rafters. Secure to the rafters using 1 1/2" roofing nails at 8" centers along the rafters. Start with afull 4 x 8 sheet, placing it flush with the bottom end of the rafters and flush with the outside edge of the first rafter. The remaining pieces will need to be cut to fill in the gaps.

8. If desired, install the brown roof edging on the outside edges of the plywood roof surface. Nail to the plywood using 1/2" roofing nails.

9. Apply asphalt building paper from the bottom up, so thatthe lower paper is overlapped by the paper above it. Staple it in placeusing a staple gun. As an added option, install brown metal roof edging to finish off the plywood roof edges. Measure and cut the pieces and install the roof edging to the edges with 1/2" roofing nails.

10. Start on either side roof, and snap a chalk line 11 1/2" up from the roof edge.

11. Trim off one-half (6") of the end tab of a shingle, using autility knife and straightedge.

12. Position the shingle upside down, so the tabs are on the chalk line and the half-tab overhangs the roof edge by 3/4". Fasten the shingle with four 1 1/2" roofing nails, about 3 1/2" up from the bottom edge: drive one below each tab, one 2" in from the edge, and one 1" from the inside edge. Drive the nails straight and set the heads just flush to avoid tearing the shingle.

13. Use full shingles for the remainder of the course, placing them upside down and butting their edges together. Trim the last shingle so it aligns with the roof edging.

14. Install the first course of shingles, starting with a full shingle. Position the tabs down and align the shingle edges with those in the starter course. Drive four nails into each shingle. Trim the last shingle to match the starter course.

15. Snap a chalk line on the building paper 17" up from the bottom edge of the first course; this will result in a 5" exposure foreach course.

16. Begin the second course with a full shingle, but overhang the end of the first course by half a tab. Begin the third course by overhanging a full tab, then 1 1/2 tabs for the fourth course. Start the fifth course with a full shingle aligned with the first course, maintaining a 5" exposure.

17. Continue this procedure until the shingles are parallel to the top ridge. Trim the top course at the ridge.

18. Repeat the same procedure to shingle the other side of the roof. Overlap the roof ridge with the top course of shingles and nail them to the outer roof side; do not overlap by more than 4 1/2".

19. Install the ridge caps. Cut ridge caps from standard shingle tabs. Taper each tab along the side edges, starting from the top of the slots and cutting up to the top edge. Cut three caps from each shingle. You will need one cap for every 5" of ridge.

20. Snap a chalk line across the shingles, 6" from the ridge. Starting at the gable ends, install the caps by bending them over theridge and aligning one side with the chalk line. Fasten each cap withone nail on each roof side, 5" from the finished (exposed) edge and 1" from the side edge. Maintain a 5" exposure for each shingle. Fasten the last shingle with a nail at each corner, and then cover the nail heads with roofing cement.

21. Trim the overhanging shingles along the gable ends. Snap chalk lines along the gable ends, 3/8" from the edges. Trim the shingles at the lines. Cover any exposed nails with roofing cement.

## APPLY FINISHING TOUCHES

1. Measure along the bottom of the top center rail and install four to five eye bolts for hanging your game. Space them evenly.

2. Using a drill and 12-inch-long, 3/8" bit, drill holes at these locations through the post.

3. Install each of the eye bolts and secure them by using washers and nuts on the top side of the center rail.

# 5

## SKINNING AND BUTCHERING GAME POLE

## TOOLS

Hand saw

Level

Tape measure

Hammer

Drill and 3/8" bit 12" long

Post hole digger

Shovel

We honestly can't take any credit for this project since we saw it at a major trade show and feel that it's a must have at any serious hunting camp. The brackets, pulley, rope, 900-pound winch, and game hanger come as a kit manufactured by Southern Outdoor Technologies, LLC. Refer to their Web site www.southernoutdoortechnologies.com for ordering information and pricing. You will also find several other products that may interest you.

We have the game pole set up directly outside our barn, but it can alsobe set up inside when the weather gets real bad since it is easily transportable. In any case, it makes skinning and butchering your deer or any big game a pleasure.

Dimensions: 13' high; 8' long; 4' wide

## CUTTING LIST

| Key | Part | Dimensions | Pcs. | Material |
|-----|------|------------|------|----------|
| A | Posts | 3 1/2" x 3 1/2" x 14' | 2 | Pressure-treated ACQ |
| B | Top rails | 1 1/2" x 5 1/2" x 8' | 2 | Pressure-treated ACQ or telephone pole |
| C | Braces | 2 1/2" x 3 1/2" x 8' | 2 | Douglas fir |

**Materials:** Hot-dipped galvanized nails, 12d, 16d; or lag bolts.

Meat Pole Kit from Southern Outdoor Technologies, LLC. (www.southernoutdoortechnologies.com)

Note: Measurements reflect the actual thickness of dimension lumber.

**Directions:** Place a 4x4 post in one end of the bracket and another one in the other side. Mount them securely to the bracket using screws provides. Repeat for the other side.

Stand both assemblies upright spaced 8' apart. You will need help from your buddy. Have someone else place the two top rails in the upper portion of the bracket. Mount to the bracket using screws. Nail the two pieces together using 12d nails.

Provide additional support to the posts, by securing a brace on each side about 3' from the bottom. Secure using several 16d nails into the posts.

Mount the pulley and rope assembly.

If the game pole is placed outside, dig around the bottom of each post to make the unit level.

Lay out locations of post holes and set posts in place.

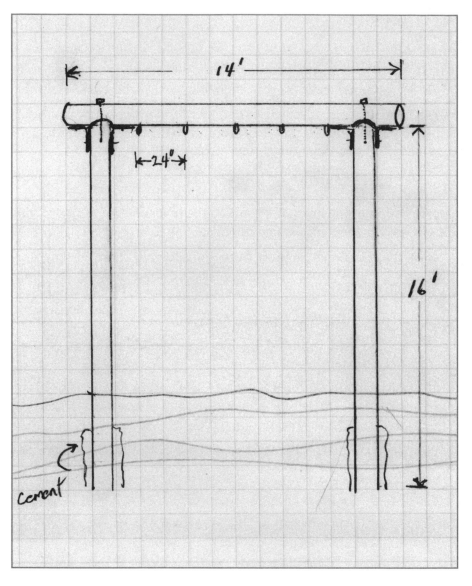

This is a simpler version of a game pole, using 8'x8' round poles.

# 6

# ARCHER'S SHED

**TOOLS**

Hand saw, circular saw, or table saw

Level

Tape measure

T-square or combination square

Screwdriver

Screw gun with Phillips head bit

Hammer

Drill with 1/4" bit

Staple gun and staples

Miter box

Sheds are a necessity, as there is never enough space for storage at any camp, farm, or home. That's why we decided to build this project specifically for storage of our archery equipment. We made it 10 feet by 10 feet and it stands 84 inches high; but, like most other projects in this book, the dimensions can easily be modified to suit your needs. The front doors open to 6 feet wide, affording plenty of space to get your equipment in and out.

During the archery season, the shed is the base of our hunting camp, where we store our practice stands, targets, tuning rack, portable tree stands, and all kinds of other equipment. We also have a workbench inside the shed with all the necessary tools for repairing our bows and arrows. Come rifle season, we relocate our archery equipment and convert this to our sighting shed.

As with many of our other outdoor projects, we recommend using Texture 1-11 siding, a hardboard, exterior siding with factory-cut vertical grooves made to simulate separate boards on a structure's exterior. T 1-11 is relatively inexpensive compared to other wood siding and takes any color stain well.

Dimensions: 84" high; 10' long; 10' wide

## CUTTING LIST

| Key | Part | Dimensions | Pcs. | Material |
|---|---|---|---|---|
| A | Railroad ties | 6" x 6" x 120" | 3 | Pressure-treated ACQ |
| B | Floor joists | 1 1/2" x 5 1/2" x 117" | 6 | Pressure-treated ACQ |
| C | Floor end joists | 1 1/2" x 5 1/2" x 120" | 2 | Pressure-treated ACQ |
| D | Floor pieces | 3/4" x 48" x 96" | 4 | Pressure-treated ACQ plywood |
| E | Front wall studs | 1 1/2" x 3 1/2" x 69" | 4 | Douglas fir |
| F | Rear/front wall plates | 1 1/2" x 3 1/2" x 120" | 4 | Douglas fir |
| G | Rear wall studs | 1 1/2" x 3 1/2" x 69" | 6 | Douglas fir |
| H | Side wall plates | 1 1/2" x 3 1/2" x 113" | 4 | Douglas fir |
| I | Side wall studs | 1 1/2" x 3 1/2" x 69" | 12 | Douglas fir |
| J | Roof rafters | 1 1/2" x 3 1/2" x 67" | 12 | Douglas fir |
| K | Gussets | 1/2" x 10" x 24" | 6 | Plywood |
| L | Roof plywood | 1/2" x 48" x 96" | 2 | Pressure-treated ACQ |
| M | Roof plywood | 1/2" x 19" x 96" | 2 | Pressure-treated ACQ |
| N | Roof plywood | 1/2" x 19" x 24" | 2 | Pressure-treated ACQ |
| O | Roof plywood | 1/2" x 24" x 48" | 2 | Pressure-treated ACQ |
| P | Side & rear wall panels | 3/8" x 48" x 72" | 6 | Exterior Texture 1-11 siding |

| Key | Part | Dimensions | Pcs. | Material |
|-----|------|------------|------|----------|
| Q | Side & rear wall panels | 3/8" x 23 7/8" x 72" | 3 | Exterior Texture 1-11 siding |
| R | Front wall panels | 3/8" x 27 3/4" x 72" | 2 | Exterior Texture 1-11 siding |
| S | Gable end panels | 3/8" x 3 11/16" x 23 9/16" x 48" | 4 | Exterior Texture 1-11 siding |
| T | Gable end panels | 3/8" x 23 9/16" x 28 1/2" | 2 | Exterior Texture 1-11 siding |
| U | Fascia trim | 3/4" x 3 1/2" x 120 3/4" | 2 | Cedar |
| V | Rear trim | 3/4" x 3 1/2" x 102 1/2" | 1 | Cedar |
| W | Gable end trim | 3/4" x 3 9/16" x 11 5/8" x 8 3/8" | 4 | Cedar |
| X | Front/rear roof trim | 3/4" x 3 1/2" x 55 7/16" | 4 | Cedar |
| Y | Corner trim | 3/4" x 3 1/2" x 72" | 4 | Cedar |
| Z | Corner trim | 3/4" x 2 1/2" x 72" | 4 | Cedar |
| AA | Door panels | 3/8 x 32" x 68 1/2" | 2 | Exterior Texture 1-11 siding |
| BB | Door frame side trim | 3/4" x 3 1/2" x 72" | 2 | Cedar |
| CC | Door trim sides | 3/4" x 3 1/2" x 68 1/2" | 4 | Cedar |
| DD | Door trim cross | 3/4" x 3 1/2" x 25" | 6 | Cedar |
| EE | Door top trim | 3/4" x 3 1/2" x 72" | 1 | Cedar |
| FF | Door stop | 1/4" x 1 1/2" x 65" | 1 | Cedar |

## Materials

Hot-dipped galvanized nails, 16d, 10d, 8d, and 6d; 1" roofing nails; 1 1/2" siding nails, 1", 6d finish nails; exterior-grade latex paint; four bundles of asphalt roofing shingles; 15# rolled asphalt paper, staples. Two 1 1/2" slide bolts, two 68" piano hinges, door handle, 4-inch hasp lock.

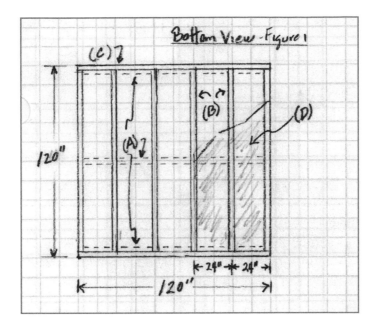

Figure 1 - Bottom View

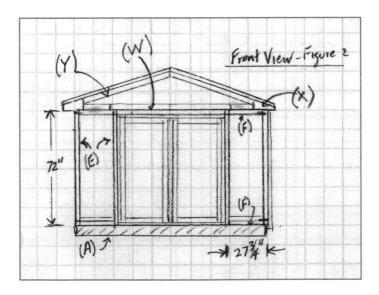

Figure 2 - Front View

Note: Measurements reflect the actual thickness of dimension lumber.

**Directions:**

**Construct the floor platform.** (See Figure 1)

1. Measure and cut pieces (A), (B), and (C) as shown in cutting list.

Lay out the three railroad ties (A) on your flat surface. Space them approximately 40" apart. If you know where the shed will be going, place them in that location. Depending on the grade, you might need to level the grade to get these posts to sit evenly.

2. Position the six floor joists (B) on top of the railroad ties (A). Two should align with the ends and the other four should be placed on 24" centers. Position the floor end joists (C) at each end of the joists (B). Secure in place by using two 10d nails at each location. Secure the platform box assembly to the railroad ties by toenailing 8d nails into the ties at each location where the joists lie on the ties.

3. Place the floor pieces (D) on top of the platform box, aligning the outside edges with the outside edges of the joists. Use two full 4x8 sheets of plywood, and place at each end of the box assembly. Cut one 4x8 sheet in half, use one half between the two full sheets and the other half at one end of the box assembly. Cut one small piece (about 2' x 2') from another 4x8 sheet and place it the last corner. Nail the plywood pieces to the joists using 8d nails. Nails should be at 6" centers.

**Construct the front and rear walls.** (See Figures 2 and 3)

1. Measure and cut pieces (E), (F), and (G) as shown in the cutting list.

Lay out the top and bottom front wall plates (F) on edge. Measure and, using a square, mark on these plates the locations of the wall studs, as shown in Figure 2. Place the four front wall studs (E) at both ends and the other two locations between (F) and nail them together with two 16d nails in each stud end.

2. Stand up the assembled front wall frame and place it on top of the front floor platform so that its outside edge is flush with the

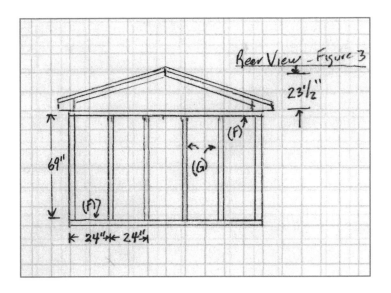

Figure 3 - Rear View

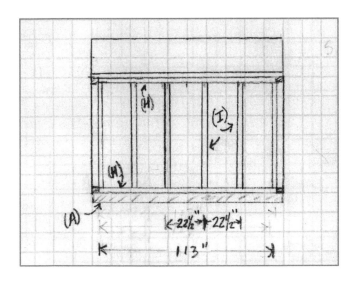

Figure 4 - Side View

41

edge of the floor. Nail it through the bottom front wall plate (F) and floor into the front floor end joist (C) using six 16d nails.

3. Lay out the top and bottom rear wall plates (F) on edge. Measure and, using a square, mark on these plates the locations of the rear wall studs, as shown in Figure 3. Place two rear wall studs (G) at both ends, and the other four at locations between (F) and nail them together with two 16d nails in each stud end.

4. Stand up the assembled rear wall frame and place it on top of the rear floor platform so that its outside edge is flush with the edge of the floor. Nail it through the bottom rear wall plate (F) and floor into the rear joist (C) using six 16d nails.

**Frame the sidewalls,** as shown in Figure 4.

1. Measure and cut pieces (H) and (I) as shown in the cutting list.

2. Lay out the top and bottom sidewall plates (H) on edge. Measure and, using a square, mark on these plates the locations of the wall studs, as shown in Figure 4. Place two sidewall studs (I) at both ends and the other four at locations between (H) and nail them together with two 16d nails in each stud end.

3. Stand up the assembled sidewall frame and place it on top of the floor platform between the front and rear wall assemblies. Nail it through the bottom sidewall plate (H) and floor into the floor joist (B) using six 16d nails.

4. Repeat Steps 1 through 3 for the other sidewall.

**Construct the roof.** Refer to Figures 4, 5, and 6.

1. Mark out the locations of roof rafters along the top side-wall plates at 24" centers using a square.

2. Place one of the roof rafters (J) on top of the sidewall so that it overhangs the side approximately 2", and the top end of the rafter is raised 23 1/2" from the sidewall plate height. Place a level against the bottom end of the rafter where it meets the sidewall plate. Make sure it reads level in the vertical direction, and mark with a pencil for the bottom plumb cut. Repeat to obtain the top plumb cut.

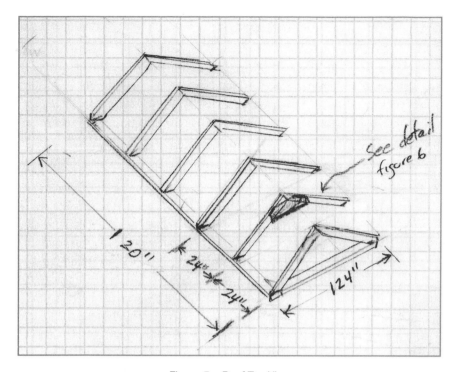

Figure 5 - Roof Top View

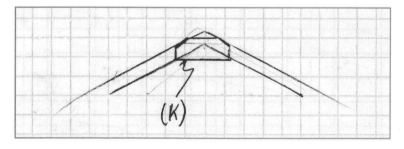

Figure 6

3. With the rafter still in position, mark the location of the bottom of the rafter where it lays on the top of the sidewall plate. Place the level in the horizontal direction and mark with a pencil for the bird's mouth level cut.

4. Using a hand saw or circular saw, cut at the locations of the bottom and top plumb cuts, and the bird's mouth level cut.

5. Use this rafter as a pattern to make the remaining 11 roof rafters.

6. Lay a set of roof rafters at one end of the shed front walls. You will need a helper to hold them in place. Using two 8d nails, toe-nail the rafters into the top wall plate at the bird's mouth locations. Nail the top plumb-cut ends of the roof rafters together by toenailing them into each other, using two 8d nails.

7. Using a gusset (K), nail to the top of the roof rafters using 1 1/2" nails.

8. Repeat Steps 6 and 7 for the remaining five sets of rafters, placing them approximately at 24" centers as marked in Step 1 above.

9. Measure and cut the plywood roof pieces (M), (N), and (O) as shown in the cutting list. Roof piece (L) is a standard-size (4x8') full sheet of plywood.

10. Place roof plywood (L) on top of the roof rafters so it is flush along one end and flush along the roof peak. Nail into the rafters using 6d nails. Nails should be placed approximately 8" along each of the rafters.

11. Place roof plywood (M) on top of the roof rafters so it is flush along the other end and butts against the bottom edge of (L). Nail it in place into the rafters using 6d nails. Nails should be placed approximately 8" along each of the rafters.

12. Place roof plywood (N) on top of the rafters so it is flush along the same edge as (L) and butts against the bottom edge of (L). Nail it in place into the rafters using 6d nails. Nails should be placed approximately 8" along each of the rafters.

13. Place roof plywood (O) on top of the remaining roof rafters so it is flush with the other end, and butts against the top edge of (M) and the end of (L). Nail it in place into the rafters using 6d nails. Nails should be placed approximately 8" along each of the rafter.

14. Repeat Steps 10, 11, and 12 for the other roof side.

**Secure siding.**

1. Measure and cut wall panels (P), (Q), (R), (S), and (T) as shown in the cutting list.

2. Secure two side panels (P) and one panel (Q) to the wall studs using 1 1/2" siding nails. Position one side panel (P) so it is flush with the wall end, the next panel (Q) in the middle, and the other panel (P) on the other end of the wall. Nail into each stud at 12" centers and along the top and bottom plates. Repeat this for the other side.

3. Repeat this same procedure for the rear wall.

4. Secure the front panels (R) to the front wall studs using 1 1/2" siding nails. Place one on each side of the door opening. Nail into each stud at 12" centers and along the top and bottom plates.

5. Secure two of the gable end panels (S) and one panel (T) to the top of the front wall using 1 1/2" siding nails. Position one panel (S) so it is flush with the wall end, the next panel (T) in the middle, and the other panel (S) on the other end of the wall. Nail into each stud at 12" centers and along the top rafter and wall plates. Repeat for the rear wall.

**Apply roof gable trim and corner trim.**

1. Secure the gable end trim (W) pieces to both ends of the front gable end. Nail in place using 6d finish nails. Repeat for the rear side.

2. Secure the front roof trim (Z) pieces to the front gable end along the roof edge. Lay in place, mark the angle where it meets the gable end trim piece (W), and the angle where both trim pieces (Z) meet at the peak, and cut using a hand saw. Nail in place using 6d finish nails. Repeat for the rear side.

3. Secure the rear trim piece (V) to the rear wall so it covers the seam where the rear wall panels meet the gable end panels. Nail in place using 6d finish nails.

4. Secure the fascia trim pieces (U) on both sides of the roof edge. Nail in place using 6d finish nails.

5. Secure the corner trim (Z) to one side so it lies flush with the front edge wall. Nail in place using 6d finish nails. Secure the other corner trim (Y) on the front wall so it is flush with the outer edge of the side corner trim (Z). Nail in place using 6d finish nails.

Repeat for the other side, and repeat for the two rear corners with the same steps.

## Apply roof shingles.

1. Apply asphalt building paper from the bottom up, so that the lower paper is overlapped by the paper above it. Staple it in place using a staple gun.

Start on either roof side and snap a chalk line 11 1/2" up from the bottom roof edge.

Trim off one-half (6") of the end tab of a shingle, using a utility knife and straightedge.

2. Position the shingle upside down, so the tabs are on the chalk line and the half-tab overhangs the roof edge by 3/4". Fasten the shingle with four 1" roofing nails, about 3 1/2" up from the bottom edge: drive one below each tab, one 2" in from the edge, and one 1" from the inside edge. Drive the nails straight and set the heads just flush to avoid tearing the shingle.

3. Use full shingles for the remainder of the course, placing them upside down and butting their edges together. Trim the last shingle so it overhangs the edge by 1/2".

4. Install the first course of shingles, starting with a full shingle. Position the tabs down and align the shingle edges with those in the starter course. Drive four nails into each shingle. Trim the last shingle to match the starter course.

5. Snap a chalk line on the building paper; 17" up from the bottom edge of the first course; this will result in a 5" exposure for each course.

6. Begin the second course with a full shingle, but overhang the end of the first course by 1/2 of a tab. Begin the third course by overhanging a full tab, then 1 1/2 tabs for the fourth course. Start the fifth course with a full shingle aligned with the first course, maintaining a 5" exposure.

7. Continue this procedure until the shingles are parallel to the top ridge. Trim the top course at the ridge.

8. Repeat the same procedure to shingle the other side of the roof. Overlap the roof ridge with the top course of shingles, and nail them to the outer roof side; do not overlap by more than 4 1/2".

9. Install the ridge caps. Cut ridge caps from standard shingle tabs: taper each tab along the side edges, starting from the top of the slots and cutting up to the top edge. Cut three caps from each shingle. You will need one cap for every 5" of ridge.

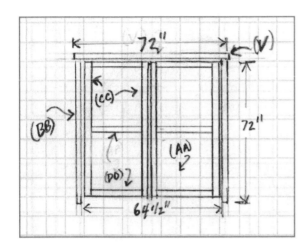

Figure 7
Door Details

10. Snap a chalk line across the shingles, 6" from the ridge. Starting at the gable ends, install the caps by bending them over the ridge and aligning one side with the chalk line. Fasten each cap with one nail on each roof side, 5" from the finished (exposed) edge and 1" from the side edge. Maintain a 5" exposure for each shingle. Fasten the last shingle with a nail at each corner, and then cover the nail heads with roofing cement.

11. Trim the overhanging shingles along the gable ends. Snap chalk lines along the gable ends, 3/8" from the edges. Trim the shingles at the lines. Cover any exposed nails with roofing cement.

**Make and install the door.**

1. Measure and cut the remaining pieces (AA) through (EE) as shown in the cutting list.

2. Trim out the doorframe using doorframe side trim piece (BB). Secure to wall studs using 6d finish nails. Install door top trim (V) above the door opening.

3. Refer to Figure 7. Secure the door trim side pieces (CC) along the sides of the door panel (AA). Nail pieces in place by driving 1" finish nails into the trim pieces from the backside of the door panel.

4. Secure the door trim cross pieces to the door panel (AA), one at the top and bottom, and the other in the middle of the panel. Nail pieces in place by nailing 1" finish nails into the trim pieces from the backside of the door panel.

5. Using the piano hinge, mount the door to the right side of the doorframe trim. The door trim should lie flush with the front doorframe trim.

6. Repeat Steps 4-6 for the left side door.

7. Install two bolts on the inside of the left side door to keep it in the closed position.

8. Place a piece of doorstop molding (FF) on the left side of the inside of the doorframe. This will provide a backstop for the door.

9. Install the handle on the right side door and the hasp lock pieces on both doors.

## APPLY FINISHING TOUCHES

1. Although it's not necessary, you may want to paint the interior surfaces. If so, use an exterior latex paint.

2. Sand smooth any rough surfaces.

3. Stain the exterior surfaces with an exterior-grade stain, or paint with the desired color.

# 7

# ARCHER'S SMALL
# STORAGE SHED

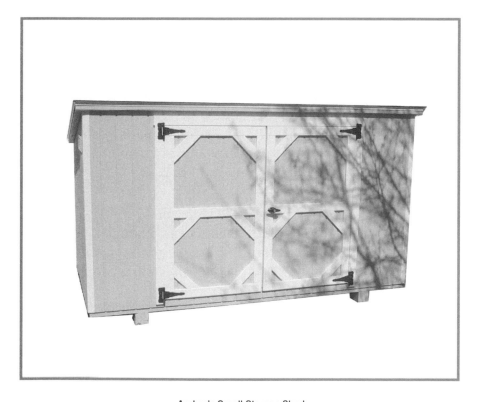

Archer's Small Storage Shed

## TOOLS

Hand saw, circular saw, or table saw

Level

Tape measure

T-square or combination square

Screwdriver

Screw gun with Phillips head bit

Hammer

Drill with 1/4" bit Staple gun and staples

Power miter box or miter box with hand saw

This small storage shed may not look like much, but believe me it is just what we needed at the camp, and maybe just what you need, too. It can be used to store anything, from your garden tools outdoor furniture, or obviously archery equipment. Although the archer's shed project in the previous chapter was built for the same reason, this one was built out of a necessity for more space to store our portable tree stands. Over the years we have managed to accumulate more than 50 portable stands and quickly ran out of space to store them. We don't like storing them outside since the weather takes a toll on them.

This shed is small enough not to require a building permit in most townships. It is light enough and relatively easy enough to move it to any location that fits the season. The basic construction techniques can be followed as described here, if you want to make the shed larger. We like this project so much that we just built another one next to the farmhouse. We needed it for storing our picnic table, chairs, and barbecue grill during the snowy winter months.

As with many of our other projects in this book, we recommend using Texture 1-11 for your siding. It is relatively inexpensive in comparison to other wood siding and takes any color stain well.

Dimensions: 74" high; 100" long; 48" wide

## CUTTING LIST

| Key | Part | Dimensions | Pcs. | Material |
|-----|------|------------|------|----------|
| A | Railroad ties | 4" x 4" x 48" | 3 | Pressure-treated ACQ |
| B | Floor joists | 1 1/2" x 3 1/2" x 96" | 4 | Pressure-treated ACQ |
| C | Floor piece | 3/4" x 48" x 96" | 1 | Pressure-treated ACQ |
| D | Front wall studs | 1 1/2" x 2 1/2" x 70" | 4 | Douglas fir |
| E | Rear/front wall plates | 1 1/2" x 2 1/2" x 96" | 5 | Douglas fir |
| F | Rear wall studs | 1 1/2" x 2 1/2" x 60" | 5 | Douglas fir |
| G | Sidewall plates | 1 1/2" x 2 1/2" x 43" | 4 | Douglas fir |
| H | Sidewall top plate | 1 1/2" x 2 1/2" x 45" | 4 | Douglas fir |
| I | Sidewall studs | 1 1/2" x 2 1/2" x 70" | 4 | Douglas fir |
| J | Roof rafters | 1 1/2" x 3 1/2" x 45" | 3 | Douglas fir |
| K | Sidewall panels | 5/8" x 48" x 77" | 2 | Exterior Texture 1-11 siding |
| L | Rear wall panels | 5/8" x 48" x 66" | 2 | Exterior Texture 1-11 siding |
| M | Roof plywood | 3/4" x 48" x 52" | 1 | Pressure-treated ACQ |
| N | Roof plywood | 3/4" x 26" x 52" | 2 | Pressure-treated ACQ |
| O | Front wall panels | 5/8" x 24" x 77" | 2 | Exterior Texture 1-11 siding |
| P | Door panels | 5/8" x 24" x 68" | 2 | Exterior Texture 1-11 siding |
| Q | Door frame top trim | 3/4" x 3 1/2" x 56" | 1 | Cedar |

| Key | Part | Dimensions | Pcs. | Material |
|-----|------|------------|------|----------|
| R | Door frame | 3/4" x 3 1/2" x 68" | 2 | Cedar side trim |
| S | Door trim sides | 3/4" x 3 1/2" x 66" | 4 | Cedar |
| T | Door trim cross | 3/4" x 3 1/2" x 17" | 6 | Cedar |
| U | Door angle trim | 3/4" x 3 1/2" x 10" | 12 | Cedar |
| V | Corner trim | 1/2" x 1" x 72" | 8 | Cedar |
| W | Doorstop | 1/4" x 1 1/2" x 65" | 1 | Cedar |

**Materials:** Hot-dipped galvanized nails, 16d, 10d, 8d, 6d, 1"; and 1/2" roofing nails, 1 1/2" siding nails, and 2d, 4d, and 6d finish nails; exterior-grade latex paint; asphalt roofing shingles; 15# rolled asphalt paper, staples; 3 x12" flat vents with wood screws. Metal roof edging, three 10' lengths; four hasp gate hinges and screws; two slide bolts, 2"; handle and latch; 3" x10" side vents; exterior-grade latex stain or paint.

Note: Measurements reflect the actual thickness of dimension lumber.

**Directions:**

**Construct the floor platform.** (See Figure 1)

1. Measure and cut pieces (A), (B), and (C) as shown in cutting list, using a hand saw or circular saw.

2. Lay out the three railroad ties (A) on your flat surface. Space them approximately 40" apart. If you know where the shed will be going, place them in that location.

3. Position the four floor joists (B) on top of the railroad ties (A). Two should align with the ends of the railroad ties and the other two should be placed on 16" centers. Secure these to the railroad ties by toenailing 8d nails into the ties at each location where the joists lie on the railroad ties.

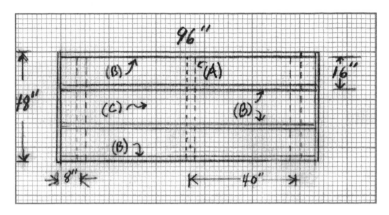

Figure 1 - Bottom

4. Place the floor piece (C) on top of the platform box, aligning the outside edges with the outside edges of the joists. Nail the plywood to the joist using 8d nails. Nails should be at 6" centers. **Construct the front and rear walls.** (See Figures 2 and 3)

1. Measure and cut pieces (D), (E), and (F) as shown in the cutting list.

2. Using two of the top front wall plates (E), nail them side- by-side using 10d nails. This will be used as your top front

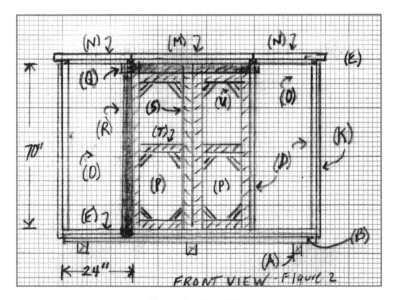

Figure 2 - Front View

53

plate. Lay out the top front plate assembly and bottom front wall plates (E) on edge. Using a square, measure and mark on these plates the locations of the wall studs, as shown in Figure 2. Place the four front wall studs (D) at both ends and the other two locations 24" from each end between top and bottom wall plates (E). Nail them together with two 16d nails in each stud end.

3. Stand up the assembled front wall frame and place it on top of the front floor platform so that its outside edge is flush with the edge of the floor. Make sure that the side-by-side top front plate is on the top. Nail it through the bottom front wall plate (E) and floor into the front joist (B) using six 16d nails.

4. Lay out the top and bottom rear wall plates (E) on edge. Using a square, measure and mark on these plates the locations of the wall studs, as shown in Figure 3. Place the two rear wall studs (F) at both ends, and the other three at 24" centers between (E) and nail them together with two 16d nails in each stud end.

5. Stand up the assembled rear wall frame and place it on top of the rear floor platform so that its outside edge is flush with the edge of the floor. Nail it through the bottom rear wall plate (E) and floor into the rear joist (B) using six 16d nails.

**Frame the sidewalls,** as shown in Figure 4.

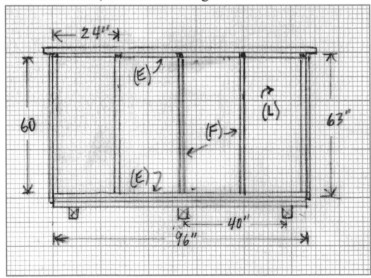

Figure 3 - Rear View

1. Lay the side bottom plate (G) between the bottom front and rear wall plates. Secure it to the plywood base by nailing three 16d nails into the floor joist.

2. Using a square, make sure the front and rear wall studs

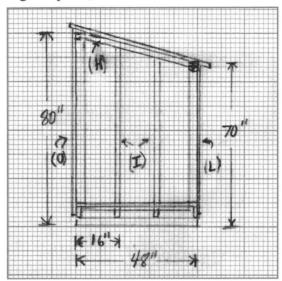

Figure 4 - Side View

are square to the bottom platform. Place the sidewall top plate (H) between the top front and wall plates and scribe the angles onto the top plate. Cut the sidewall top plate at both locations using a hand saw.

3. Use this as a pattern, and cut the other sidewall top plate (H). You should also use this same piece as a pattern to cut the roof rafters (J). The only exception is that the angle for the roof rafters should be cut along the wider end of the 2x4 studs.

4. Position the sidewall top plate in place between the top front and rear wall plates. Secure it to the wall by toenailing with 8d nails. Repeat this for the other sidewall.

5. Place two of the sidewall studs (I) at 16" center and scribe along the top of the studs. Make the angle cut using a hand saw. Secure it in place by nailing two 10d nails into the top and toenailing two 8d nails into the bottom plate. Repeat this for the other sidewall.

6. Place one of the sidewall panels (K) against the sidewall, with the edge flush with the front wall stud. Trace on the backside of

the panel along the roof rafter. Using a hand saw or jigsaw, cut the angle. Secure it to the sidewall studs using 1 1/2" siding nails. Nail into each stud at 12" centers and along the top and bottom plates. Repeat this for the other side.

**Construct the roof.** Refer to Figure 5.

1. Using a square, mark out the locations for roof rafters along the top front and rear wall plates at 16" centers.

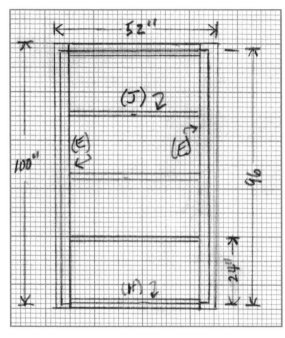

Figure 5 - Top View

2. Place a roof rafter (J) between the top front and rear wall plates at the 24" center. Secure it in place by toenailing at both ends using 8d nails. Repeat this for the remaining two rafters.

3. Measure and cut the plywood roof pieces (M) and (N) as shown in the cutting list.

4. Place roof piece (M) on top of the three cen-ter roof rafters so it overhangs evenly on the front and top wall edges. Nail it in place into the rafters using 6d nails. Nails should be placed approximately 8" along each of the raft-ers.

5. Place the two other roof pieces (N) on each side of the roof rafters. Nail it in place into the rafters using 6d nails. Nails should be placed approximately 8" along each of the rafter.

**Apply roof shingles.**

1. Install white metal roof edging along all four edges of the plywood roof. Secure to the plywood using 3/4" roofing nails.

2. Apply asphalt building paper from the bottom up, so that the lower paper is overlapped by the paper above it. Staple it in place using a staple gun.

3. Snap a chalk line 11 1/2" up from the rear roof edge.

4. Trim off one-half (6") of the end tab of a shingle, using a utility knife and straightedge.

5. Position the shingle upside down, so the tabs are on the chalk line and the half-tab overhangs the roof edge by 3/4". Fasten the shingle with four 3/4" roofing nails, about 3 1/2" up from the bottom edge: drive one below each tab, one 2" in from the edge, and one 1" from the inside edge. Drive the nails straight, and set the heads just flush to avoid tearing the shingle.

6. Use full shingles for the remainder of the course, placing them upside down and butting their edges together. Trim the last shingle so it overhangs the edge by 1/2".

7. Install the first course of shingles, starting with a full shingle. Position the tabs down and align the shingle edges with those in the starter course. Drive four nails into each shingle. Trim the last shingle to match the starter course.

8. Snap a chalk line on the building paper; 17" up from the bottom edge of the first course; this will result in a 5" exposure for each course.

9. Begin the second course with a full shingle, but overhang the end of the first course by 1/2 of a tab. Begin the third course by overhanging a full tab, then 1 1/2 tabs for the fourth course. Start the fifth course with a full shingle aligned with the first course, maintaining a 5" exposure.

10. Repeat this procedure until the roof is covered. Trim the shingles along both edges.

**Secure the siding to the rear and front walls.**

1. Measure and cut the front and rear wall panels (L) and (O) as shown in the cutting list.

2. Place one of the rear wall panels (L) against the rear wall, with one edge flush with the edge of the sidewall siding. Secure it to

the rear wall studs using 1 1/2" siding nails. Repeat this procedure for the other rear wall panel.

3. Place one of the front wall panels (O) against the front wall, with one edge flush with the edge of the sidewall siding. Secure it to the front wall studs using 1 1/2" siding nails. Repeat this procedure for the other front wall panel.

**Make and install the door.**

1. Measure and cut the remaining pieces (P) through (V) as shown in the cutting list. Cut door angle trim pieces (U) at 45-degree angles using a hand saw and miter box or a power miter box.

2. Trim out the doorframe using doorframe top and side trim pieces (Q) and (R). Secure to wall studs using 6d finish nails.

3. Referring to Figure 2, secure the door trim pieces (S), (T), and (U) to the door panels (P). Nail pieces in place by driving 2d finish nails into the trim pieces from the backside of the door panels.

4. Using the hasp gate hinges, mount the door to the right side of the doorframe trim. The door trim should lie flush with the front door frame trim.

5. Repeat this for the left side door.

6. Install two bolts on the inside of the left side door to keep it in the closed position. Install one on the bottom and the other on the top side of the inside door.

7. Place a piece of doorstop molding (W) on the left side of the inside of the doorframe. This will provide a backstop for the door.

8. Install the handle and latch on the right side door.

## APPLY FINISHING TOUCHES

1. Although it's not necessary, you may want to stain or paint the interior surfaces. If so, use an exterior latex stain or paint.

2. Sand smooth any rough surfaces.

3. Add trim (V) as desired on the four vertical corners. Secure using 2d finish nails.

4. Stain the exterior surfaces using exterior stain or paint of the desired color.

5. Using a jigsaw, cut out an opening near the top of the side, close to the roof ridge for the vent. Use a 1/4" drill to drill a hole in the corner to start the cut. Screw into the siding using wood screws. Repeat for the other side.

6. Move the shed to its desired location if you did not build it in place.

Archer's Small Storage Shed
--back and side view--

The Premier Tree Stand is almost finished. We used the aluminum ladder (underneath) to apply camo paint to the underside of the tree stand and to secure the 3/8" threaded rods to the trees.

# 8

# PREMIER
# TREE STAND

This stand was designed to be large and sturdy, which also makes it heavy. The platform is large and strong enough to accommodate two adults quite comfortably. The archer's premier stand allows you to invite either a beginning hunter or a non-hunting companion (a child, wife, spouse, or friend) with you to experience the excitement of your hunt, or anyone you'd like to accompany as they take their deer as well. In any case, the archer's premiere tree stand provides enough platform space for two to sit safely and comfortably during the hunt.

This stand incorporates a 3/8" threaded rod that is about 3 to 4 feet long that fits around at least two tree trunks and is then secured tightly with 3/8" nuts and washers. The stand must be attached to healthy, tall trees with a main trunk of sizeable diameter (at least 18 inches). We like to attach this stand to a group of oaks. It should be set in a group of trees (at least three or four) or one very large tree with a few good sized trunks growing from it. Although the rear platform measures 48" in width, the tree stand can be mounted to wider trees since the rear platform measures 72" wide.

This tree stand is one of our favorite designs because it is also intended to give you more height than many tree stands. The height of the platform is approximately 15 feet, when using 16-foot side rungs. Since 2x4s are not readily available in longer lengths, making the platform any higher is not possible unless you want to extend the side rungs by bolting two pieces together. However, we do not recommend that since doing this lessens the overall strength of the stand and makes it very cumbersome and heavy to move.

Although it is most definitely intended to be mounted in one spot as a longtime stand, with some time and effort it can be removed and relocated, if absolutely necessary, by removing the mounting bolts and rods used to secure it to the tree. Unlike smaller and lighter designs, however, this stand will require up to two or three strong people to move it to another location.

We try locating a fairly large group of trees so the base can be mounted to two separate limbs. This also requires you to find only a spot with one solid, good-sized tree trunk for setup.

For this stand and any other stand we build, we strongly recommend that it be constructed from pressure-treated ACQ wood, including all rails, steps, braces, and supports. If built from pressure-treated wood, this stand will withstand the weight of two adults and remain strong and durable over the years, as long as you also check it at least twice a year to make sure none of the components needs to be secured or replaced.

Dimensions: 14' high; 48" wide; 48" long; ladder steps 25" wide

## CUTTING LIST

| Key | Part | Dimensions | Pcs. | Material |
|-----|------|------------|------|----------|
| A | Ladder tree steps | 1 1/2" x 3 1/2" x 25" | 12 | Pressure-treated ACQ |
| B | Ladder side rails | 1 1/2" x 3 1/2" x 16' | 2 | Pressure-treated ACQ |
| C | Rear platform support | 1 1/2" x 5 1/2" x 72" | 1 | Pressure-treated ACQ |
| D | Front platform support | 1 1/2" x 5 1/2" x 36" | 1 | Pressure-treated ACQ |
| E | Side platform supports | 1 1/2" x 5 1/2" x 46" | 2 | Pressure-treated ACQ |
| F | Platform decking | 3/4" x 48" x 48" | 1 | Pressure-treated ACQ- plywood |
| G | Ladder/ Platform supports | 1 1/2" x 3 1/2" x 62" | 2 | Pressure-treated ACQ |
| H | Ladder tree supports | 1 1/2" x 3 1/2" x 65" | 2 | Pressure-treated ACQ |
| I | Safety railing supports | 1 1/2" x 3 1/2" x 42" | 4 | Pressure-treated ACQ |
| J | Side railings | 1 1/2" x 3 1/2" x 49" | 2 | Pressure-treated ACQ |
| K | Front railing | 1 1/2" x 3 1/2" x 40" | 1 | Pressure-treated ACQ |
| L | Seat support | 1 1/2" x 3 1/2" x 48" | 1 | Pressure-treated ACQ |
| M | Seat platform | 3/4" x 16" x 48" | 1 | Exterior plywood |
| N | Seat brace | 1 1/2" x 3 1/2" x 16" | 1 | Pressure-treated ACQ |
| O | Optional deck supports | 1 1/2" x 5 1/2" x 45" | 2 | Pressure-treated ACQ |

## Directions:

**Materials:** Hot-dipped galvanized nails, 16d, 10d; 1 1/2", 2 1/2", and 3" wood deck screws; 20d nails and/or hooks; 20' nylon rope; 3/8" x 6" carriage bolts, nuts, and washers; two 4-foot lengths of 3/8" threaded rod, washers, and nuts. Two wooden wedges (1 1/2" x 2" x 1/4"). Camouflage burlap, three pieces 48" x 48".

Note: Measurements reflect the actual thickness of dimension lumber.

**Construct the ladder.** (See Figures 1 and 2)

1. Cut the ladder steps (A) to size as shown in the cutting list, using a hand saw or circular saw.

2. Lay out the two ladder rails (B) on edge on a flat surface. Measure the distance between each step, and mark the edges of each side rail. The actual spread of the steps can be made to vary, depending on your size and comfort level. You will find that the older you get, the closer together you'll want to the ladder steps. For this particular design, using steps that are 3 1/2" wide, the spread between steps was made at approximately 12-13", for a total of 12 steps.

3. Secure each step to the side rails by nailing one 16d nail in the center of the step to the rail on each side. If you have access to an air powered nail gun, I highly recommend its use. It will save you lots of time and energy as you are nailing the stand pieces together and to the trees.

4. Provide additional support to the steps by using 3" wood screws. Screw two screws on each side of each step and repeat for both side rails.

**Construct the platform.** (See Figure 3).

1. Cut the remaining pieces (C), (D), (E), (F), and (G) to size using a hand saw or circular saw as shown in the cutting list.

2. Lay out the two side platform supports (E) on edge on a flat surface approximately 48" apart. Place the rear platform support (C) at the ends of the side platform supports. Make sure that the ends overlap the side supports by approximately 16" on each side. Secure together by nailing a 16d nail into the ends of the side platform support. Provide additional support by screwing at least two 3" screws into each end.

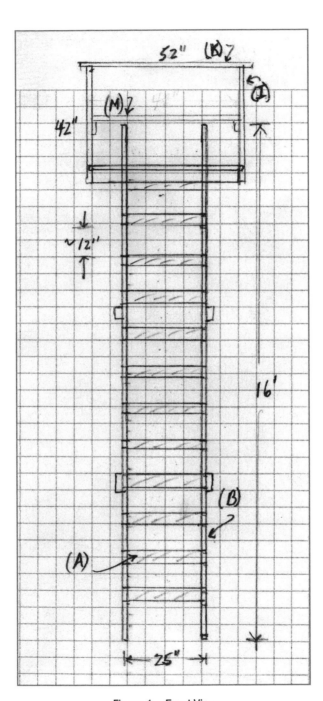

Figure 1 - Front View

65

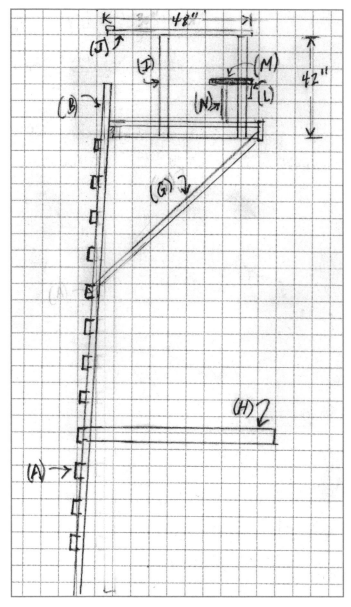

Figure 2 - Side View

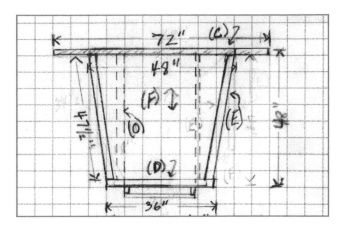

Figure 3 - Top View

3. Place the front platform support (D) at the front end of the side platform supports. Secure together by nailing a 1d nail from the front into the ends of the side platform support. Provide additional support by screwing at least two 3" screws into each end. (Author's note: The ends of the side platform supports can be cut at a slight angle to makc for a closer fit against the rear and front platform supports.)

4. Lay the platform decking (F) on top of the finished platform support with the rear flush with the outside edge of the rear platform support. Mark the underside of the platform to match the support frame. Using a circular saw, jigsaw, or hand saw, cut out the finished shape of the platform. Place it back on the frame and secure the platform decking (F) to the side and rear platform supports using 1 1/2" nails or screws into the platform support frame edges.

5. As an added option, install two deck supports in the bottom side of the platform. Place them centered 24" apart. Secure them to the front and rear platform supports using 16d nails. Use 1 1/2" nails or screws and secure the platform into the two supports.

**Assemble the ladder to the platform.** (See Figures 2 and 3).

1. Lay out the platform on end on a flat surface. Place the assembled ladder on the front platform support, so that the ladder extends past the top of the platform by approximately 14".Temporarily support the other end so the ladder is at a slight angle with the

platform. Position it so that it sits evenly between the front platform supports.

2. Drill two 3/8" holes through the ladder side rail through the front platform support about 2 1/2" apart. Repeat for the other side.

3. Secure the ladder to the platform with two 3/8" x 6" carriage bolts, nuts, and washers on each side. Slip a small wooden wedge (1 1/2" x 2" x 1/4") on each side where the bottom of the front platform support meets the ladder side rails. Tighten the nuts using a socket or open-end wrench.

4. Make sure that the ladder is at a slight angle to the platform.

5. Cut the ends of the platform angle supports (G) at 45-degree angles using a hand saw.

6. Place one of the supports against the inside of the rear bottom of the platform and the other end so it just overlaps the ladder side rail. Secure it in place by using at least three 2 1/2" wood screws at each location. Repeat for the other support.

**Mount the tree stand, safety railing, and seat.** (See Figures 2 and 3)

1. Pick out the location and trees you want to use for your tree stand. For this stand, we like to look for a grouping of trees with at least two solid main trunks side-by-side, which provides a sturdy footing for mounting the platform.

2. You will need at least three people to erect this stand and secure it against the tree. Have two people pick up the platform from both sides, with the bottom of the ladder on the ground. Start walking it up off the ground. The third person, on the opposite side of the trees, can pull up on a piece of rope tied to the rear platform support.

3. A fourth person could brace their feet on the bottom of the ladder to prevent it from slipping while grabbing and pulling up toward the tree by grabbing the steps. If a fourth person is not available, make sure that the bottom of the ladder is wedged up against the bottom of the tree base.

4. Now that the platform back edge is against the trees, level off the platform by moving the ladder out away from the tree trunk. Have one person lean against the front of the ladder, putting pressure on the platform against the tree trunk. If a rope was used to pull up from the backside of the trees, tie it around another tree to hold the platform in place temporarily.

5. Have one person carefully and slowly climb the ladder with a couple of 3" wood screws and a screw gun. Screw into the back of the rear platform support into the trees. For additional strength and support, use a four-foot length of 3/8" threaded rod on each end. Predrill two sets of 3/8" pilot holes on both sides of the rear platform support. The holes should be spaced at least 14" apart so they align slightly wider than both sides of the tree trunk. These holes will be used for the 3/8" threaded rods.

6. Bend the threaded rod into shape around the backside of the tree, placing both ends into the predrilled holes in the rear platform support. Place washers and nuts and tighten up the nuts until the platform is secured tightly to the trees. Repeat for the other side with another length of threaded rod.

7. Secure two of the safety railing supports (I) on one side of the side platform supports. Place the first one on the tree end and the second one at the front edge of the platform. Secure to the side platform supports using three 3" wood screws in each end. Repeat this for the other side.

8. Place one of the side railing (J) pieces on the top ends of the side railing supports (I). Secure in place by screwing two 3" wood screws into each end. Repeat this for the other side.

9. Place the front railing (K) on the front ends of the two side rails (J). Secure in place at both ends by screwing two 3" screws into the side rails.

10. There are a variety of seats that can be used for this type of tree stand. We have found that a bench seat mounted across the backside against the two trees works best and affords you the most versatility. Secure the seat support (L) against the trees at 17" from the base of the platform. This piece can also be mounted between the rear side railing supports (I).

11. Place the seat platform (M) on top of the seat support (L). Secure it in place by screwing five 3" screws into the seat support.

12. Place the seat brace (N) in the middle of the seat platform in the front. Secure it to the seat by screwing two screws into the seat brace end. Secure the other end of the seat brace into the platform decking by toenailing 2" screws.

## APPLY THE FINISHING TOUCHES

1. For additional support, secure the ladder tree support (H) approximately 50" from the base of the tree stand. One end should be screwed into the side of the ladder side rail, and the other end into the tree using at least three 3" wood screws at each location. Repeat for the other side.

2. Using several different colors of exterior spray paint (brown, black, and green), paint the tree stand steps, platform, and railing so the tree stands blends in with the trees.

3. Use hooks or 20d nails, placing several of them at heights above the platform to hang your bow, gun, and other hunting equipment.

4. Measure and cut a piece of nylon cord and secure it to the top of the platform to be used to pull up your bow or gun safely from the ground. Never climb a tree stand while holding a bow or gun.

5. For additional concealment when in the tree, wrap the platform area with camouflage burlap. Simply staple it to the top side and front railing with a staple gun.

6. Using a chain saw, hand pruning saw, or pole saw, trim out any overhanging branches or limbs from around the tree stand location.

This is how we used the threaded 3/8" rods to attach the tree stand to the tree. We repeated the process with the tree stand and the other tree next to this one.

# 9

# QUICK AND EASY
# TREE STAND

When you find two trees spaced apart just like these two - it's easy to build your own simple tree stand. Here we are finishing the floor.

## TOOLS

Chain saw, hand pruning saw, pole saw

Hand saw, circular saw

Cordless drill

Screw gun and bits

Air-powered gun with 16d nails

Torpedo level

Well, it doesn't get much easier than this tree stand design. True to its name, this one is quick and easy to set up. It requires a minimal amount of wood for the small platform and seat, and does not require any wood for the steps, since access to the platform is made through the use of screw-in steps or removable pegs. We have also shown how to build and mount a ladder with steps, for those of you who might feel more comfortable climbing a ladder rather than screw-in steps or pegs. It is so easy that Peter was able to build this one by himself (okay, not actually by himself—he needed the assistance from his amazing son Cody, and the director Katie).

We do not recommend this one for novice hunters, because the platform is small and offers very little protection in the fall. The seat is small, but large enough to be comfortable and a comfortable seat is what I would recommend that you have for this stand.

It can literally be built in less than two hours. Simply find a few tree spread apart by 3–4 feet and you are in business. We have built several of these on the farm, and tend to use them as scouter stands, erecting one of these in an area that we want to scout. If the area proves to be a good one, we tend to follow up by building one of our more solid designs.

We have provided three options for the steps. Simply use the screw-in steps, removable step bolts, or—if you are looking for more comfort and ease in climbing—construct and install the ladder as described.

The removable step bolts are a great choice when constructing a platform in an area where others may be able to hunt, and you don't want to make it too easy for someone else to climb into the stand. Step bolts are also good to use if you have several different platforms, where you don't want to provide permanent steps. Simply carry the step bolts in your fanny pack, use them to climb into the stand, and remove them as you descend the stand at the end of your hunt.

These step bolts are available from E-Z KUT Hunting Products (www.woodyhunting.com).

They are easily installed using Woody's Convertible Hand and Cordless Drill bit. The step bolts, hand drill, and bit come in a convenient case. We also strongly recommend the use of the E-Z UP Climbing System when drilling the holes, installing/removing the step bolts as you climb or descend the stand. This climbing belt can be worn either right- or left-handed. It is adjustable to fit anyone in your camp, whether they are thin or on the heavy side. It is by far the most comfortable, safest, and most adjustable climbing belt we have ever used. In fact, we keep several extra climbing belts at our camp for our guests. For insurance reasons and to assure the utmost in safety for our guests, we require them to use a climbing belt when climbing any of our stands. All hunters at our camp understand and follow our safety rules. E-Z UP Climbing System belts are highly recommended when setting up or removing portable platform tree stands, as well as when hunting.

Last but not least, this climbing belt makes a great deer drag belt. Simply fasten the belt around your waist, extend the rope to the desired length, and tie the end around the head of your deer or the end of your Game Sled. Now you can walk and drag your trophy to your vehicle or camp.

Once the stand is erected, prune the trees and branches. Besides the use of an extendable pole pruning saw, we recommend the use of the E-Z KUT Hunting Products heavy-duty ratchet pruner.

Dimensions: 15'high; 18" wide; 36" long

## CUTTING LIST

| Key | Part | Dimensions | Pcs. | Material |
|-----|------|------------|------|----------|
| A | Platform supports | 1 1/2" x 5 1/2" x 58" | 2 | Pressure-treated ACQ |
| B | Platform | 1 1/2" x 3 1/2" x 18" | 8–10 | Pressure-treated ACQ |
| C | Seat brace | 1 1/2" x 3 1/2" x 16" | 1 | Pressure-treated ACQ |
| D | Seat platform | 3/4" x 15" x 15" | 1 | Exterior plywood |
| E | Seat support | 1 1/2" x 3 1/2" x 17" | 1 | Pressure-treated ACQ |
| F | Ladder Tree Steps | 1 1/2" x 3 1/2" x 26" | 13 | Pressure-treated ACQ |
| G | Ladder side rails | 1 1/2" x 3 1/2" x 16' | 2 | Pressure-treated ACQ |
| H | Safety railing | 1 1/2" x 3 1/2" x 58" | 1 | Pressure-treated ACQ |

**Materials:** Hot-dipped galvanized nails, 16d, 1 1/2", 2 1/2"; wood deck screws, 3"; 20d nails and/or hooks; 20' nylon rope; 10–14 screw-in steps; 10–14 step bolts, available from E-Z KUT Hunting Products (www.woodyhunting.com).

Note: Measurements reflect the actual thickness of dimension lumber.

### Directions:

Cut all pieces to the desired lengths as shown in the cutting list, or to the proper lengths depending on your chosen tree.

### Install screw-in steps, step bolts, or wooden ladder.

1. Install screw-in steps. This is the easiest approach. If you prefer to use a ladder, skip this step and proceed to Step 3, below.

A. Depending on the desired height of the platform, screw the tree steps one at a time into the tree trunk. Space them approximately 12–14" apart or whatever makes it comfortable for you to climb.

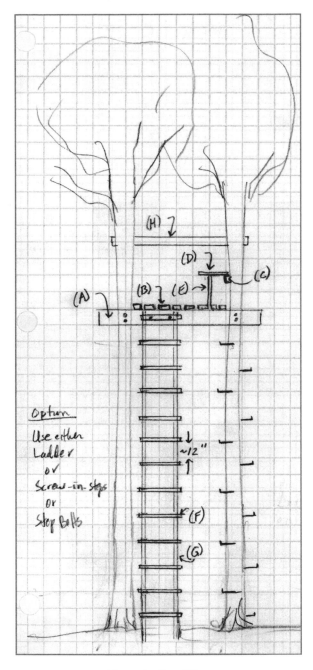

Figure 1 - Front View

75

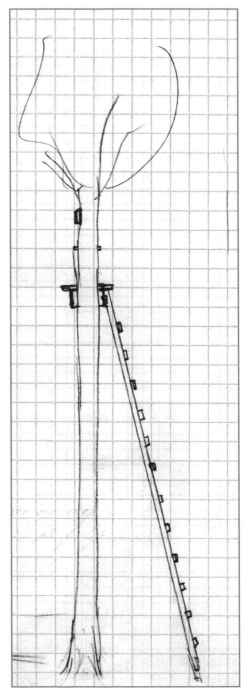

Figure 2 - Side View

B. When installing the screw-in steps, make sure that you use a safety belt.

C. To make screw-in steps a bit easier to install, I suggest that you use a cordless drill and predrill 1/4" holes, approximately 1" deep.

2. Install step bolts. This approach is great when you want easy access to your stand and to deter others from using it. You install the pegs as you climb the stand, and remove them as you descend at the end of your hunt. The steps can be installed using a hand drill with a bit or a cordless power drill with bit.

A. Using the hand drill, place the heel of your left hand against the tree and grasp the hand drill by its collar with your thumb underneath and your first and middle fingers on the top of the collar. Angle the drill bit down slightly—this will prevent the step bolts from falling out.

B. Exert just enough inward pressure to start the drill; the drill bit is self-feeding and requires no inward pressure while drilling the hole. Don't try to change the bit's cutting angle; the self-feeding tip is very hard and may break off. If you're not happy with the angle or placement, remove the bit and start over at a different location.

C. When the bit reaches the proper depth, it will stop drilling. At that point, you will feel the last wood chip break; continue turning the drill a few more times, then grasp the drill by the handle with the bit between your first and middle fingers and pull the bit straight out; there is no need to turn the drill backwards. Pulling the bit out will pull out the wood chips. As you climb the tree, just leave the hand drill and bit in the last highest hole to free up both hands so you can raise up your safety belt, then step up to a higher Bolt Step.

3. Slide in your Woody Step Bolts.

Using the Convertible Cordless Drill Bit (these instructions are provided with kit):

A. Place the drill bit in the chuck of your cordless drill. Angle the bit downward slightly and exert slight inward pressure to start the bit cutting. Then just support the drill so the bit doesn't bind; the bit is self-feeding and will pull itself into the tree that you are drilling.

B. When the bits stops cutting just run the drill for a few seconds then pull the drill bit out of the tree. Flick out the chips from the bit flutes before starting another hole. (Authors note: As you ascend the tree it is imperative that you use a safety climbing belt. We highly recommend the use of the E-Z UP Climbing Belt available from www.ezkutpruners.com.)

C. As you are ascending up the tree just leave the drill and the bit in the last highest hole to free up both hands so you can raise up your safety belt and step up higher on the step bolts.

D. Slide in your Woody Bolt Steps as you go up.

**Construct the ladder** (optional).

1. Cut the ladder steps (F) to size as shown in the cutting list, using a hand saw or circular saw.

2. Lay out the two ladder rails (G) on edge on a flat surface. Measure the distance between the steps and mark the edges of each side rail. The actual spread of the steps can vary, depending on your size and comfort level. You will find that the older you get, the closer you will want the steps to be. For this particular design, using steps that are 3 1/2" wide, the spread between each step was made at approximately 12" for a total of 12 steps.

3. Install the last step at the top on the back side of the side rails.

4. Secure each step to the side rails by nailing one 16d nail in the center of the step to the rail on each side. If you have access to an air-powered nail gun I highly recommend its use. It will save you lots of time and energy as you are nailing the pieces together and to the trees.

5. Provide additional support to the steps by using 3" wood screws. Screw two screws on each side of each step and repeat for both side rails.

**Construct the platform and install the ladder.** (Author's note: As you construct the platform, it is imperative that you use a safety climbing belt. We highly recommend the use of the E-Z UP Climbing Belt.)

1. Measure the distance between the outsides of the two trees at the location of the platform. For our tree stand, this distance was 48". Therefore the length of the platform supports (A) should be made 4–5" longer on each end, or in our case 58".

2. Position yourself up the tree, either on the tree steps or using an extension ladder. Get help from your partner to hold the platform in position as you mount it to the trees. When using the ladder, make sure that it is safely tied to the tree at the top step. Using two 16d nails, secure it to the tree. Use at least two 3" wood screws for additional support into the tree. For additional support, use one 3/8" x 5" lag bolt in each end and tighten using a ratchet or hand wrench. Repeat this for the other end into the other tree trunk. Using a torpedo level, make sure that the platform support is level.

3. If you have access to an air-powered nail gun, I highly recommend its use. It will save you lots of time and energy as you are nailing the pieces to the trees.

4. Repeat this same procedure making sure that both sides of the platform supports are at the same height. Place a board across the mounted support and use a torpedo level to align both sides.

5. Secure the platform (B) pieces one at a time by screwing two 3" wood screws into the platform supports at each side. They should overhand each side by 1–2".

6. Repeat Step 4 for each platform piece, spacing them apart by 1". For our tree stand, the inside distance between the two trees was 34", therefore we used eight pieces spaced approximately one 1" apart.

7. If a ladder was constructed, mount it to the stand. It can be mounted on either side of the platform. Secure it to the platform by using several 3" screws through the top back step into the base of the platform.

## Complete seat and safety railing

1. Place the seat brace (C) against the side of the tree where you want the seat, approximately 17" from the bottom of the platform. Secure it to the tree by using three 3" screws into the tree.

2. Position the seat platform (D) on top of the seat brace (G) and secure it by drilling four 1 1/2" decking screws into the brace.

3. Place the seat support (E) in the middle of the front of the seat. Screw the seat bottom to the seat support by screwing two 2 1/2" screws in the top end of the seat support. Secure the bottom of the seat support to the bottom platform by using a 2 1/2" wood screw, and toenail it into the platform. Note: Another option is to assemble the

seat on the ground, hoist it up with a rope, and then install in to the tree and the platform as described above.

4. Place the safety railing (H) in place against the tree stumps approximately 40" from the base of the platform. Secure in place by using three screws into the tree on each side.

## APPLY FINISHING TOUCHES

1. Using several different colors of exterior spray paint (brown, black, and green), paint the platform and seat so the tree stand blends in with the trees.

2. Place hooks or 20d nails at heights above the platform to hang your bow, gun, and other hunting equipment.

3. Measure and cut a piece of nylon cord and secure it to the top of the platform to be used to pull up your bow or gun safely.

4. Using a chain saw, hand pruning saw, or pole saw, trim out any overhanging branches or limbs from around the tree stand location. (Author's note: When hand pruning we highly recommend the use of an E-Z KUT Hunting Products heavy-duty ratchet pruner.)

# 10

# ULTRALIGHT WRAP GROUND BLIND

Here is a do-it-yourself camo ground blind that looks like a permanent blind. This one weighs about twenty-five pounds and can be moved from one location to another by just two people. It is ideal for bowhunting in warmer weather.

## TOOLS

Circular saw or hand saw and miter box

Level

Tape measure

T-square or combination square

Screwdriver

Cordless screw gun

Hammer

Drill and bits

Wood clamps

Staple gun and 3/8" staples

This ground blind is one of my personal favorites. Why? Simply put, it's one of the easiest yet one of the most practical and affordable blinds we have made. It can easily be modified in height and width to meet your desire and application, depending upon how many others are expected to sit in the blind with you. It can be built in sections in your barn or garage, transported on a small trailer or RTV, and quickly assembled in the field once you have decided on your secret spot. Or it can be built whole, then easily transported to your favorite spot.

The blind is made of 2x2 ACQ strips of wood, enclosed in a manufactured camo blind wrap material available from Omnova Solutions, Inc. This camo blind wrap is a durable, heavy-duty, yet lightweight vinyl material. It offers scent containment and sound-deadening properties that make it an ideal solution for these types of blinds. It is wind-, water-, fade-, and tear-resistant, as well as mold- and mildew-resistant (refer to www.omnova.com). If you desire different patterns, you can contact the company directly for possibility of different patterns. This particular blind is built with an optional reinforced plywood floor and roof for protection from rain or snow.

The windows used in this blind are pre-manufactured windows sold as kits available from www.shadowhunterllc.com. We highly recommend their use for self-made blinds. If you have preexisting blinds, it is relatively simple to modify the blinds to make use of these window kits. They are relatively inexpensive and are extremely practical, simple to install, and quiet during hunting outings. Obviously, the design of these windows suits archers, but they are available for gun hunters as well. The window openings are the same size, but lie horizontally rather than vertically. You might also want to make use of both window styles, the archery style and the gun style. The instructions for installation, along with photos, are included with the kit and have been repeated in this chapter to show you why these are the windows of choice.

If cost is a big factor, instructions have been provided to simply use Plexiglas mounted with piano hinges. One last warning: Although it makes use of a very durable material we don't guarantee it withstanding a fallen heavy branch or tree, which can puncture the material.

Dimensions: 76" high; 72" long; 48" wide

## CUTTING LIST

| Key | Part | Dimensions | Pcs. | Material |
|-----|------|------------|------|----------|
| A | Floor joist | 1 1/2" x 3 1/2" x 72" | 2 | Pressure-treated ACQ |
| B | Floor joist | 1 1/2" x 3 1/2" x 45" | 5 | Pressure-treated ACQ |
| C | Plywood floor | 3/4" x 4' x 6' | 1 | Pressure-treated ACQ |
| D | Vertical supports | 1 1/2" x 1 1/2" x 72" | 8 | Douglas fir |
| E | Horizontal side supports | 1 1/2" x 1 1/2" x 42" | 8 | Douglas fir |
| F | Horizontal front/ rear supports | 1 1/2" x 1 1/2" x 69" | 7 | Douglas fir |
| G | Rear window supports | 1 1/2" x 1 1/2" x 43 1/2" | 2 | Douglas fir |
| H | Window supports | 1 1/2" x 1 1/2" x 22 3/8" | 8 | Douglas fir |
| I | Corner braces | 1 1/2" x 1 1/2" x 12" | 24 | Douglas fir |
| J | Roof support | 1 1/2" x 3 1/2" x 72" | 1 | Douglas fir |
| K | Plywood Roof | 3/4 x 48 1/4" x 72" | 1 | Pressure-treated ACQ |

| Key | Part | Dimensions | Pcs. | Material |
|-----|------|------------|------|----------|
| L | Roof frame F/R | 1 1/2" x 1 1/2" x 75" | 2 | Douglas fir |
| M | Roof frame sides | 1 1/2" x 1 1/2" x 45" | 2 | Douglas fir |
| N | Plywood door | 3/4" x 23 1/2" x 68 1/2" | 1 | Pressure-treated ACQ |
| O | Door frame supports-vertical | 3/4" x 2" x 72" | 2 | Pressure-treated ACQ |
| P | Door frame supports-horizontal | 3/4" x 2 x 23" | 2 | Pressure-treated ACQ |
| Q | Bottom window supports | 1 1/2" x 1 1/2" x 30" | 8 | Douglas fir |
| R | Windows | 1/4" x 10 x 25" | 3 | Plexiglas |

**Materials:** Hot-dipped galvanized nails, 6d siding nails; 1 1/2", 2 1/2", and 3" wood deck screws; three 3" barn hinges; hasp lock; two barrel bolts; camouflage mesh; brown or black exterior-grade paint. Optional, if pre-manufactured windows are not used: Plexiglas for windows; stainless steel 8/32 x 1/2" machine screws, nuts, and washers; three 10" or 20" piano hinges; four hook-and-eye latches; one roll of Hidden Timber Camo Blind Wrap (covers 4' x 6' x 8') available from www.omnova.com; four Silent Shadow Archer Windows and hardware kit, available from www.shadowhunterllc.com.

Note: Measurements reflect the actual thickness of dimension lumber. Windows part (R) are needed only if pre-manufactured windows from Shadowhunter are not used.

**Construct the floor**. (See Figure 1)

   1. Measure and cut pieces (A), (B), and (C) as shown in cutting list.

   2. Lay out the two floor joists (A) on edge on your work surface. Place the two floor joists (B) at both ends between (A) and nail them together with 16d nails.

   3. Nail three floor joists (B) spaced evenly (18" apart) between the two joists (A).

   4. Place the floor piece (C) on top of the platform box, aligning the outside edges with the outside edges of the joists. Nail the plywood to the joist using 6d nails.

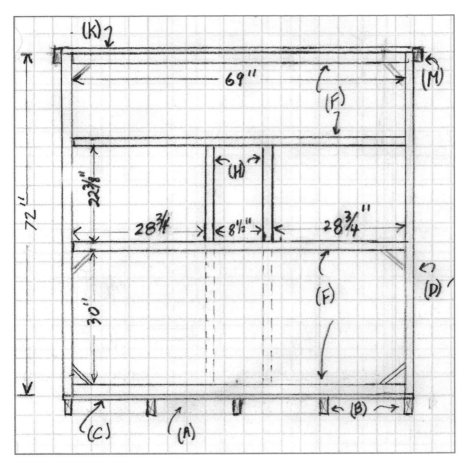

Figure 1 - Front View

**Assemble the front frame.** (See Figure 1)

1. Measure and cut pieces (D), (E), (F), (G), (H), and (I) as shown in the cutting list.

2. Work on a flat surface such as a workbench or table set up with a piece of plywood and lay out two vertical supports (D) approximately 69" apart.

3. Place four horizontal front supports (F) between supports (D). One should be at the top, one at the bottom, one 30" from the bottom, and another one 53 7/8" from the bottom. These last two supports are for your window openings, which can be adjusted to meet your particular design or style.

85

4. Secure together by using two 3" decking screws at each joint. To make it easier, use a drill with a 1/8" bit and predrill pilot holes through the horizontal supports. Screw in place using a screw gun.

5. Place two window supports (H) approximately 8 1/2" apart between the two middle horizontal supports (E). They should be placed about 28 3/4" from each side. Secure in place using 3" decking screws.

6. Using a square, square each corner and install the braces (I) at the locations shown in Figure 1. Secure the braces using two 3" decking screws at each joint.

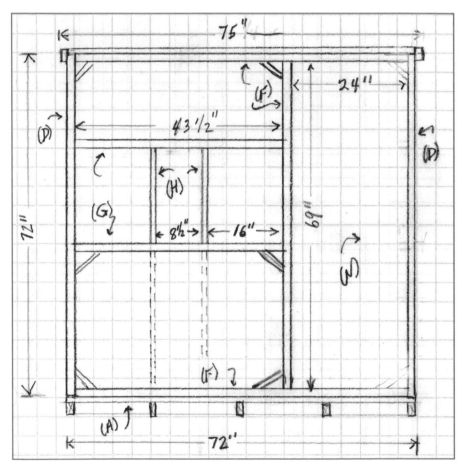

Figure 2 - Rear View

**Assemble the rear frame** (see Figure 2).

1. Lay out two vertical supports (D) approximately 69" apart.

2. Place two horizontal rear supports (F) between supports (D). One should be at the top and one at the bottom.

3. Secure together by using two 3" decking screws at each joint. To make it easier, use a drill with a 1/8" bit and predrill pilot holes through the horizontal supports. Screw in place using a screw gun.

4. Place a horizontal rear support (F) between the top and bottom rear support (F) at 24" from the right side of rear panel. This door can be placed on the opposite side if desired. Secure in place using two 3" decking screws at each joint.

5. Place two window supports (G) between the vertical support (D) and the rear support (F), one 30" from the bottom, and another one 53 7/8" from the bottom. 6. Secure in place using 3" decking screws.

6. Place two window supports (H) approximately 8 1/2" apart between the two window supports (G). They should be placed approximately 16" from each side. Secure in place using 3" decking screws.

7. Using a square, square each corner and install the braces (I) at the locations shown in Figure 2. Secure the braces using two 3" decking screws at each joint.

**Assemble the sides** (see Figure 3).

1. Work on a flat surface such as a workbench or table set up with a piece of plywood and lay out two vertical supports (D) approximately 42" apart.

2. Place four horizontal front supports (F) between supports (D). One should be at the top, one at the bottom, one 30" from the bottom, and another one 53 7/8" from the bottom. These last two supports are for your window openings, which can be adjusted to meet your particular design or style.

3. Secure together by using two 3" decking screws at each joint. To make it easier, use a drill with a 1/8" bit and predrill pilot holes through the horizontal supports. Screw in place using a screw gun.

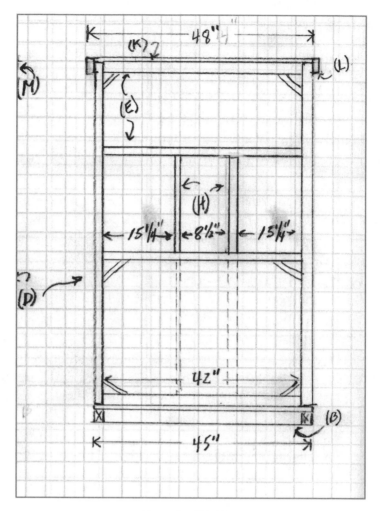

Figure 3 - Side View

4. Place two window supports (H) approximately 8 1/2" apart between the two middle horizontal supports (E). They should be placed approximately 15 1/4" from each side. Secure in place using 3" decking screws.

5. Using a square, square each corner and install the braces (I) at the locations shown in Figure 1. Secure the braces using two 3" decking screws at each joint.

## Assemble the frame structure.

1. Place the four completed wall sections on top of the finished plywood deck.

Stand up the front frame and both side frames on the inside of the front frame corner post (i.e., the front section is outside the side sections. Using wood clamps, temporarily clamp the frame at both corners. Place the rear frame on the other side outside the side frame. Clamp in place as above.

2. Secure together by using four 3" decking screws along the corner posts. Repeat for the remaining three corner sections. Remove the wood clamps.

3. Position the frame so that the bottom horizontal supports lie flush with the four edges of the finished plywood deck. Secure to the deck using three 3" decking screws into the plywood deck.

## Wrap the blind with the material and cut windows.

1. Start at the door opening and wrap the vinyl camo material around the frame. Start at the inside of the door support and staple the vinyl in place. Leave approximately 1/2" extra along the top edge of the frame assembly.

2. Maintain the vinyl tight as you pull it around the rear frame, wrap around the side, stapling along the bottom floor joists and top horizontal supports. Continue wrapping and stapling until you get it around the front frame and the other side frame. Cut and wrap the vinyl so it fits around the inside of the other side of the door opening. Staple in place.

3. Fold the excess vinyl material over the top horizontal supports and staple in place along the inside edges.

4. Using a sharp utility knife, make a cut in the center of each window. Cut from the center diagonally into each of the four corners of the window.

5. From the inside of the blind, wrap the vinyl around the window frame and staple to the inside of the frame. Cut off the excess material using the utility knife.

6. Cover any exposed wood using pieces of the excess wrap. For the pieces above and below the door opening, install a 24" piece and wrap and staple it around the inside of the wood.

## Assemble the roof.

1. Place the roof supports (J) between the two side frames in the middle of the top horizontal supports. Secure in place using two 3" decking screws at each joint.

2. Lay out the plywood roof (K) on top of the frame structure. Align the outside edges of the plywood with the frame front, rear, and sides.

3. Secure in place by screwing 1 1/2" decking screws along the plywood edges into the top frame pieces.

4. Position the roof frame side (M) against the edge of the plywood on one side so that it lies flush with the top roof surface. Secure in place using 2 1/2" decking screws. Repeat for the other side.

5. Position the roof frame piece (L) against the front edge of the plywood so that it lies flush with the top roof surface. Secure in place using 2 1/2" decking screws. Repeat for the rear.

6. Paint the roof top and frame pieces using brown or black exterior-grade paint.

7. If desired, instead of painting the top, wrap the plywood roof assembly with the camo wrap and staple in place along the outside edges of the roof frame pieces.

## Install door and windows.

1. Lay the door (N) on a flat surface. Use adhesive to attach the vinyl wrap to the outside surface of the plywood. Wrap the excess vinyl around the edges of the door. Staple along the inside surface of the door and cut any excess using a utility knife.

2. Attach three hinges to the door, approximately 6" from the top and bottom, and one in the middle.

3. Attach the door hinges to either side of the vertical door support, depending on which way you prefer the door to open.

4. Measure and cut the door back supports, one for each vertical side and one for the horizontal top and bottom openings of the door. Secure these in place by using several 1 1/2" decking screws along the edge.

5. Attach hasp lock in middle of the door, and attach a barrel bolt approximately 6 inches below the hasp. Also, attach a barrel bolt on the inside to keep the door closed when you are hunting from the

blind. (Author's note: This project used custom-designed windows manufactured by Shadow Hunter LLC (www.shadowhunterllc.com). Considering their practicality and low cost, we highly recommend their use. They are available in the archery style for vertical opening or in a gun style, for horizontal opening.)

6. Install the Four Silent Shadow Archer Windows. Although directions are provided along with the window kits, we have repeated these directions in this book. Refer to Appendix A for step-by-step detailed steps, with photos explaining how to install them. Additional bottom window supports (Q) need to be installed under each window opening for mounting of these windows. Use two supports (Q) directly below the window supports (H) by toe nailing 2 1/2" decking screws on each end. They should be spaced 8 1/2" apart.

7. If the Shadow Hunter Archery windows are not used, mount piano hinges to the bottom or side of each window (R), depending on how you prefer the window to open. Drill holes in the Plexiglas to match up with the holes in the hinges. Use 8/32 x 1/2" screws, nuts, and washers and mount the hinges to the window along the edge. Mount the other side of the hinge to the inside of the window frame. Use wood screws to mount to the wood.

8. Install latches on the opposite side of the hinges from the Plexiglas to secure the windows closed when not in use.

9. You may also want to install some camouflage mesh to provide shielding while looking through the open windows. Simply staple the mesh to the top wooden frame and allow it to hang down with the window opened.

## APPLY FINISHING TOUCHES

1. Place the blind in the desired locations. Depending on the grade, you may have to place bricks or treated lumber in the corners to level out the blind.

2. Hang a few hooks inside the blind to hang your equipment.

3. You can also make a small shelf or two and mount in the corners.

4. Place a small chair inside, or use a five-gallon bucket for your seat.

This blind looks out over one of my favorite spots that includes several waterholes, a stream, and a small food plot. The large conifer behind the blind helps to lessen the overall profile of the structure.

# 11

# ELEVATED CONDO BLIND

## TOOLS

Circular saw or hand saw

Jigsaw

Level

Tape measure

T-square or combination square

Screwdriver

Cordless screw gun

Hammer

Drill and bits

We decided to build this blind based upon some manufactured enclosed blinds that we set up on the farm; the reason was simply a matter of dollars and cents. The premade blinds that we set up were quite costly, where this blind was no more than 30 percent as much, plus we could make it to our specifications. No doubt, some of those manufactured blinds may last a bit longer, but make no mistake, ours will last at least 20 years, as long as we maintain a protective coat of stain or paint on the exterior-grade wood. One last benefit is that this blind could be manufactured in our barn and then assembled out in the field, making it easier to transport the materials a little at a time, especially considering the remote locations of some of our blinds.

It is large enough to comfortably seat at least two people and provide the capability for some great videos and photographs. In fact it is large enough to set up a cot if you really want to get an edge, by getting in the blind early and taking a nap until sunrise. Leo's brother Ralph has been proposing to do this for the last three years, but to date he has been all talk and no action. Perhaps one of these days he will surprise us all and give it a try.

Windows were installed on three sides, affording us views of the dominant travel routes. Depending on the time of day and the known travel patterns, the windows can be kept closed. The windows were made large enough to comfortably shoot a bow.

We used all exterior pressure-treated ACQ for the frame and outside supports, and exterior-grade plywood for the roof and the siding. We stained it for both protection against the weather and to help conceal it against the natural background of the large pine tree that it sits against. The roof can be finished with a layer of asphalt-based roof coating, or pieces of asphalt rolled roofing with edges sealed with asphalt sealant. This will provide additional waterproofing and extend the life of the roof indefinitely.

Dimensions: 14' high; 72" long; 48" wide

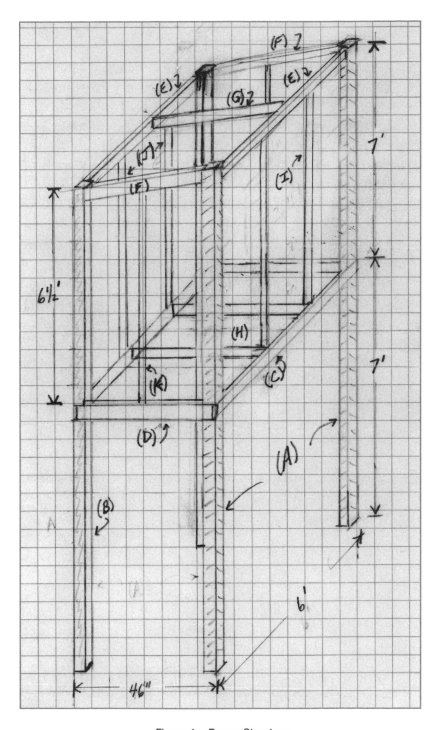

Figure 1 - Frame Structure

## CUTTING LIST

| Key | Part | Dimensions | Pcs. | Material |
|-----|------|------------|------|----------|
| A | Front corner posts | 3 1/2" x 3 1/2" x 14' | 2 | Pressure-treated ACQ |
| B | Rear corner posts | 3 1/2" x 3 1/2" x 13 1/2' | 2 | Pressure-treated ACQ |
| C | Front/rear floor joists | 1 1/2"x 5 1/2" x 72" | 2 | Pressure-treated ACQ |
| D | Floor joists | 1 1/2" x 5 1/2" x 43" | 4 | Pressure-treated ACQ |
| E | Front/Rear roof joists | 1 1/2" x 3 1/2" x 72" | 2 | Pressure-treated ACQ |
| G | Mid roof joist | 1 1/2" x 3 1/2" x 43" | 1 | Pressure-treated ACQ |
| H | Floor platform | 3/4" x 46" x 72" | 1 | Pressure-treated ACQ plywood |
| I | Front wall studs | 1 1/2" x 2 1/2" x 67 3/4" | 2 | Pressure-treated ACQ |
| J | Rear wall studs | 1 1/2" x 21/2" x 61 3/4" | 2 | Pressure-treated ACQ |
| K | Side wall studs | 1 1/2" x 2 1/2" x 64 1/4" | 2 | Pressure-treated ACQ |
| L | Rooftop | 3/4" x 48 x 76" | 1 | Pressure-treated ACQ plywood |
| M | Top front siding | 3/4" x 42 x 73 1/2" | 1 | Pressure-treated ACQ plywood |
| N | Bottom front siding | 3/4" x 48 x 73 1/2" | 1 | Pressure-treated ACQ plywood |
| O | End siding | 3/4" x 46 x 96" | 2 | Pressure-treated ACQ plywood |
| P | Rear siding | 3/4" x 42 x 73 1/2" | 2 | Pressure-treated ACQ plywood |
| Q | Various supports | 1 1/2" x 3 1/2" x 8–10' | 6-8 | Pressure-treated ACQ |
| R | Window/door supports | 1 1/2" x 1 1/2" x 8' | 3 | Pressure-treated ACQ |

| Key | Part | Dimensions | Pcs. | Material |
|-----|------|------------|------|----------|
| S | Ladder rails | 1 1/2" x 3 1/2" x 8' | 2 | Pressure treated ACQ |
| T | Ladder steps | 1 1/2" x 3 1/2" x 24" | 6-7 | Pressure-treated ACQ |

**Materials:** Hot-dipped galvanized nails, 6d siding nails, 1 1/2", 2 1/2", and 3" wood deck screws; two 4" hinges; Three 20" piano hinges; five hook-and-eye latches; hasp and lock; three barrel bolts; camouflage mesh; exterior-grade camo latex stain or paint; optional Plexiglas for windows; optional roll roofing or asphalt roof coating.

Note: Measurements reflect the actual thickness of dimension lumber.

**Construct the frame structure** (see Figure 1).

1. Measure and cut pieces (A), (B), (C), (D), (E), (F), (G), (H), (I), (J), and (K) as shown in cutting list, using a circular saw or hand saw.

2. Lay out one of the front corner posts (A) on a flat surface. Measure up from the bottom of the front post and scribe marks at 66 1/2" and 72", respectively. Make the same marks on another outside corner.

3. Using a circular saw, cut out notches 1 1/2" deep about 1/2" apart within these marks on both outside corners. Using a hand chisel and hammer, notch out the cutouts. This will provide you with a corner post with the two outside corners notched out for the front and side floor joists.

4. Repeat this same procedure (Steps 2 and 3) for the other three corner posts. The following steps will require help from your buddy.

5. Lay out two front corner posts (A) on edge on your work surface. Place them approximately 72" apart on edge with the notches facing up. Place the front floor joist (C) in the notched cutouts so that the ends of the front floor joist are flush with the outside corners. Secure them to the post by using four 3" wood screws into each end.

97

6. Lay out the two rear corner posts (B) and repeat the same procedure as above using the rear floor joist (C).

7. Stand up the rear post assemble in the vertical position. Have your Buddy hold it in the upright position. Stand up the front post assembly approximately 46" apart.

8. Place one of the floor joists (D) in the side notched cutouts so that the ends are flush with the front/rear floor joists. Secure them to the post by using four 3" wood screws. Repeat this for the other side.

9. Position the two remaining floor joists (D) between the front and rear floor joists at 24" centers. Secure them in place by screwing three 3" screws into the end of each joist.

10. Notch out the corners of the floor platform (H) by measuring 3 1/2 x 3 1/2' squares and use a hand saw to make the cutouts. Lay the floor platform on the floor joists. Secure it in place by using 1 1/2" wood screws into the floor joists and front and rear floor joists.

11. Place the front roof joist (E) between the inside of the front corner posts so that it is flush with the top ends of the posts. Using 2 1/2" wood screws secure this joist by screwing in at an angle into the corner posts (same principle as toenailing except that you are using screws). Repeat this for the rear roof joist (E).

12. Make sure that the corner posts are square with the floor platform on both sides. Place one of the end roof joists (F) between the side corner posts at the top and scribe the angles of the end roof joist. Using a hand saw, cut the angle on both ends. Use this as a pattern for the other side end roof joist, trace the angles and cut both ends. Place one of the joists so that it is flush with the top ends of the corner posts. Using 2 1/2" wood screws, secure this joist by using three 2 1/2" wood screws at angles into the corner posts. Repeat this for the other side.

13. Place the mid-roof joist (G) in the middle of the front/rear roof joists. Secure it in place by driving three 3" wood screws into the ends.

14. Position the two front wall studs (I) 22" from each front corner post. Secure them in place by using three 2 1/2" screws into the floor platform and into the front roof joist. (This will leave a 28" space between the two front wall studs for cutout of the front window.)

15. Position the two rear wall studs (J) 24" from each rear corner post. Secure them in place by using three 2 1/2" screws into the floor platform and into the rear roof joist. (This will leave a 24" space between the two rear wall studs for cutout of the rear entry door.)

16. Position the sidewall stud (K) midway between the two side corner posts. Secure it in place by using three 2 1/2" wood screws into the floor platform and into the side rear joist. Repeat this for the other side.

**Secure the siding and roof** (see Figures 1 through 4).

1. Measure and cut the remaining pieces (L), (M), (N), (O), and (P) as shown in the cutting list, using a circular saw.

2. Position the end siding (O) on one end. Have your buddy hold it in place so that the top of the siding overhangs the top of the end roof joist (F). Trace the angle cut along the backside of the end siding. Cut the angle using a circular saw. Secure it to the sidewall studs and corner posts using 1 1/2" nails at 8" centers along the studs and posts. This piece will overhand the side floor joist by approximately 10". Repeat this for the other side.

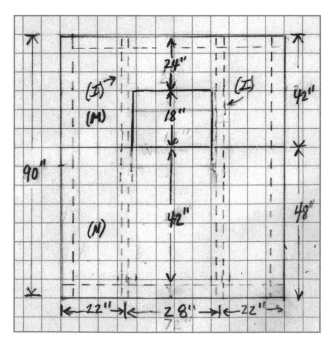

Figure 2 - Front View

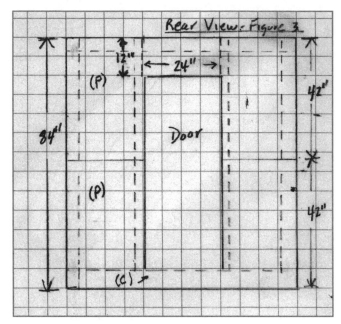

Figure 3 - Rear View

3. Position the top front siding piece (M) on the front studs so that it is flush with the top of the front roof joist. Secure it to the studs and corner posts by using 1 1/2" nails at 8" centers along the studs and corner posts. Place the bottom front siding (N) up against the top piece. Secure it in place in same manner.

4. Before closing in the blind, decide on the locations of your windows. For this blind, we wanted a window in the front and a window in each of the sidewalls. The rear wall is for the access door. The wall studs were installed such that they will provide the edges of the window frame. From the inside of the blind, measure down approximately 24" from the top roof between the two front wall studs. Drill a 1/4" hole in each corner of the studs at this 24" line. Measure down from these holes approximately 18" and make two more holes in each corner. Use a straightedge and pencil to connect the holes outlining the windows. From the outside of the blind, use a jigsaw to cut along the lines (vertically along the studs) and horizontally to make the rectangular window. Set aside for now. Repeat this same procedure for each of the side windows, except that the holes will be placed between the middle wall stud and the front corner post.

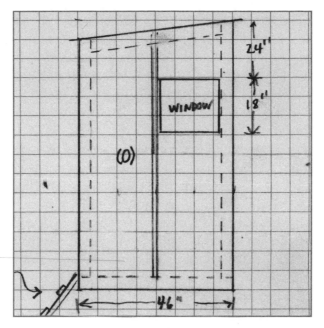

Figure 4 - Side View

5. Secure the rear siding (P) as stated in Step 3 above.

6. Place the rooftop (L) on the roof joists so it overhangs evenly on the sides and front and rear walls. Nail into place by using 1 1/2" nails into the front, rear, side, and mid-joists at 8" centers.

7. Climb into the blind through the front window to make the cutout for the access door. Measure approximately 12" from the top roof between the two rear wall studs. Drill two more holes on the bottom where the studs meet the floor platform. Use a straightedge and pencil to connect the holes outlining the door. From the outside of the blind, use a jigsaw to cut along the lines (vertically along the studs) and horizontally along the top and bottom to make the rectangular door. Set aside for now.

**Complete the door and windows and access ladder.**

1. Stiffen up the door and window cutouts previously cut in Steps 4 and 7 above by framing the inside edges with 1 1/2" x 1 1/2" stock. Secure in place around the edges with 1 1/2" wood screws.

2. Mount the door to the frame using two 4-inch hinges on the outside. Follow the manufacturer's instructions on installing the hinges. The hinges can go on either side, depending on how you prefer the door to swing open. Install a hasp on the outside of the door so the blind can be locked when not in use. On the inside, install two hook-and-eye latches so you can secure the door closed from the inside when occupied.

3. Mount the windows to the front and side surfaces. Place a piece of 1 1/2" x 1 1/2" stock along the inside of the top edge of the window cutouts. Secure it in place by driving 1 1/2" wood screws from the outside. The windows can now be hinged from the inside by using piano hinges screwed along the top edges of the windows and this stock piece. Install barrel bolts from the inside so the windows can be left closed when not in use. Install an hook-and-eye latch on the top edge of each window so you can keep the window open when you're inside. Another option is to use pieces of Plexiglas windows on hinges inside. In either case, I would suggest that you cover the window openings with camouflage mesh.

4. Make an 8-foot ladder using two ladder rails (S) and six or seven 24" ladder steps (T). Screw the top rungs to the side of the back of the blind just under the bottom of the door.

## APPLY FINISHING TOUCHES

1. Since this blind stands off the ground by 7 feet, I highly recommend that it be supported with 2x4 cross pieces. Provide this support by crossing the front and sides with bracing into the ground in both directions. Secure the braces to the main post using 3" wood screws, and wedge the ends into the dirt. Additional support can be provided by tying 1/16" stainless steel wire around the post and staked into the dirt using tent spikes.

2. Although it's not necessary, you may want to stain or paint the interior surfaces. If so, use an exterior-grade latex paint.

3. If you did not use rolled roofing or asphalt roof coating, the roof should be stained or painted with an exterior-grade stain or paint.

4. Stain or paint the exterior walls with and exterior stain or paint with the desired colors, making a camo pattern to match the surroundings.

This shows how we secure the window when it's open. By having the window swing inside to open, there is no movement outside the blind that can be detected by deer.

Our movement in and out of the blind is partially concealed by the large conifer behind the stand.

The Boot Storage Bench is a practical project that will help keep your entranceway free from the clutter of hunting boots.

# 12

# BOOT STORAGE BENCH

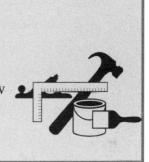

This bench provides not only a comfortable place to sit, but also storage for your boots after a day's hunt. The boots can be placed directly in the cubby hole or you can purchase individual straw baskets to store the boots in. We used poplar, since we wanted to finish it with an enamel paint. If you plan to stain or varnish it, use another wood such as pine or oak. You might also want to buy a few pillows to place on top of the bench for a bit more comfort.

This unit also doubles as a terrific place to store hats, gloves, and other loose items after a day's hunt. We each take one cubby to avoid mixing our stuff. If you leave your boots outside, there is even more storage room below the seats. It can be placed in a mud-room, but since it is pleasing to the eyes, it can also be used inside as well.

If need be the bench can be made wider or taller. We used straw baskets to help conceal any boots or other unsightly hunting clothes from view. In a real-guy type camp, you could use plastic or wooden boxes under the bench, or just throw the boots, gloves, and hats under the seat.

It will also keep the cleaning of mud and dirt from your boots at a minimum. We liked this project so much that we built another one of treated lumber and have it outside on the covered porch.

Dimensions: 21" high; 52" long; 16" wide

## CUTTING LIST

| Key | Part | Dimensions | Pcs. | Material |
|-----|------|------------|------|----------|
| A | Top Seat | 3/4" x 16" x 50" | 1 | Poplar plywood |
| B | Bottom shelf | 3/4" x 16" x 50" | 1 | Poplar plywood |
| C | Bench Sides | 3/4" x 16" x 21" | 2 | Poplar plywood |
| D | Middle dividers | 3/4" x 16" x 16 1/4" | 2 | Poplar plywood |
| E | Bottom molding | 3/4" x 4" x 52" | 1 | Poplar |
| F | Bottom sides | 3/4" x 4" x 17" | 2 | Poplar |
| G | Top trim | 3/4" x 1 1/2" x 52" | 1 | Poplar |
| H | Top Side trim | 3/4" x 4" x 17" | 2 | Poplar |
| I | Top back trim | 3/4" x 4" x 52" | 1 | Poplar |

Materials: Wood glue, 2" galvanized wood screws; 6d finishing nails; 8  feet of 3/4" self-adhesive edge trim; optional cushions; optional baskets, 15" square 9-10" high.

Note: Measurements reflect the actual thickness of dimension lumber.

**Directions:**

Measure and cut pieces (A), (B), (C), and (D) using a table saw from a piece of 4x8 poplar plywood 3/4" thick, as shown in the cutting list.

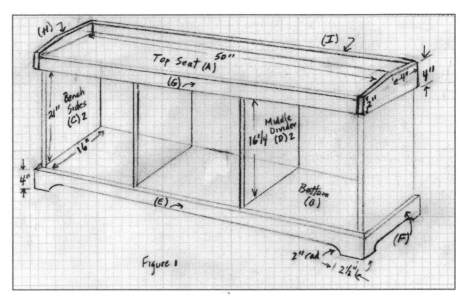

Figure 1 - Boot Storage Bench

1. For bench sides (C), cut the bottom shape as shown in Figure 1, using a jigsaw. Measure 2 1/2" from each bottom end, mark a 2" radius and then cut out the shape.

2. Measure and cut pieces (E), (F), (G), (H), and (I) from 3/4" x 5" poplar using a table saw as shown in the cutting list.

**Assemble all the pieces.**

1. Attach the sides (C) to the bench top seat (A), using wood glue and three wood screws on each side. The screws should be driven flush with the side surface.

2. Position the bottom shelf (B) so that it is 4" from the bottom of the sides. Using wood glue and three wood screws in each side, secure the sides to the bottom shelf. These screws used in Steps 1 and 2 will be covered with the trim.

3. Place the two middle dividers (D) between the top seat (A) and bottom shelf (B) evenly spaced between the sides. Use wood glue and three screws from the bottom of the bottom shelf and secure in place. Nail through the top seat three 6d finish nails into each of the middle dividers.

4. Using a miter box and hand saw or a power miter box, cut 45-degree angles on the corners of the bottom molding piece (E) so it fits along the front bottom. Cut the same 45-degree angle on each of the bottom sides (F). Place in position and cut square the opposite ends so the pieces are flush with the back of the bench sides. Secure the bottom molding piece and the bottom sides using wood glue and 6d finish nails.

5. Using a jigsaw, cut the shape of the bottom molding and sides, as shown in Figure 1. Measure 2 1/2" from each end, mark a 2" radius, and then cut the shape.

6. Secure the top trim (G) to the top of the top seat using wood glue and seven 6d finishing nails into the top seat edge. The top edge of the trim should be flush with the top surface of the top seat.

7. Cut the shape of the top side trim pieces, as shown in Figure 1. Secure both top side trim pieces (H) to the bench sides using wood glue and three 6d finish nails. These pieces should extend up past the top of the top seat, and the bottom should be even with the lower edge of the top trim.

8. Secure the top back trim (I) to the rear of the top seat edge using wood glue and seven 6d finishing nails.

9. Using a heated iron, attach the 3/4" edge trim on the front edge of the sides and the middle dividers. This provides a finished edge.

## APPLY FINISHING TOUCHES

1. Set the finish nails below the wood surfaces with a nail set.

2. Fill all visible holes with wood putty.

3. Sand the entire surface using a palm sander.

4. Paint to your desired color. I suggest using a semi-gloss or high-gloss paint. Two coats should be applied after applying a primer coat of paint. Sand lightly between each of the last few coats of paint.

# 13

# ARCHER'S STORAGE BOX

| TOOLS |
|---|
| Table saw |
| Drill |
| Screw gun |
| Router with a 3/4" rabbet bit |

Thishis box is made large enough to hold your bowhunting accessories such as arrows, broadheads, target tips, fletching, glue, vanes, and miscellaneous tools. The upper section, when opened, has a convenient removable storage tray that I use for all my tools.

Handles on each side of the box make it easy to carry and can alsobe used to secure it to your ATV

Since we wanted a painted finish, we used poplar, a relatively in expensive wood, which takes a few coats of paint well. Other woods such as pine or oak could be used if you are looking for a wood-grainfinish.

It was finished with exterior-grade hunter green paint, and then painted in a camouflage pattern using brown and black paint.

Dimensions: 12 3/4" high; 13" deep; 36" wide

## CUTTING LIST

| Key | Part | Dimensions | Pcs. | Material |
|---|---|---|---|---|
| A | Top | 3/4" x 13" x 36" | 1 | Poplar |
| B | Front and back | 3/4" x 12" x 36" | 2 | Poplar |
| C | Sides | 3/4" x 12 1/4" x 12" | 2 | Poplar |
| D | Bottom | 3/4" x 12 1/4" x 34 1/2" | 1 | Poplar |
| E | Tray bottom | 3/4" x 11 1/4 x 34 1/4" | 1 | Plywood |
| F | Tray sides | 3/4" x 2" x 9 3/4" | 2 | Poplar |
| G | Tray front/back | 3/4" x 2" x 34 1/4" | 2 | Poplar |
| H | Handle | 3/4" x 2" x 11 1/4" | 1 | Poplar |

**Materials:** Wood glue; one 16" long piano hinge (1/2") with screws; lock hasp; 10" #10 brass plumber's chain; two handles; 4d and 6d finish nails; 1 1/2" #6 flathead wood screws; wood putty; finishing materials, such as paint; two pieces of foam.

Note: Measurements reflect the actual thickness of dimension lumber.

**Directions:**

Measure and Cut all the pieces (A), (B), (C), and (D) as shown in cutting list.

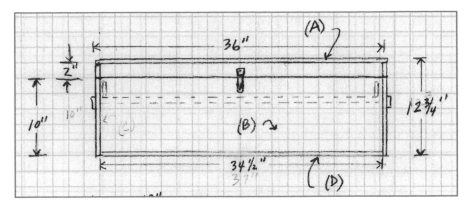

Figure 1 - Front View

1. Cut pieces (A) through (D) to desired lengths and widths with a table saw. Lay out and cut the rabbet joints on the front and back pieces (B) along the inside of the ends. This can be done in several different ways depending on the tools you have. The most accurate tool to use is a router with a 3/4" dado bit and a side guide. Set the depth of the router bit 3/8" deep, and set the guide so you cut the edges 3/4" wide. Lay the boards on your workbench and run the router along the entire edge. Repeat for the back piece.

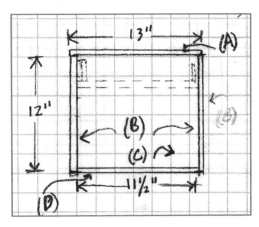

Figure 2 - End View

2. Lay out and cut the rabbet joints on the inside of the bottom of the front and back (B), and side pieces (C).

**Assemble all the pieces.**

1. Attach the side pieces (C) to the front and back pieces (B). Start the 6d nails through one side of the rabbet joint until the ends just protrude on the inside. Apply some wood glue to the joint. Position the side piece into the joint of the front, then, resting the opposite end of the side on the bench, drive the nails in. Attach the other side in the same manner and repeat this for the back piece to complete the box.

2. Attach the bottom piece (D) to the sides (C) and front and back (B). Apply glue to the rabbet joints at the bottom of the sides, front, and back. Put the bottom in place. Drill starter holes and screw three #6 flathead wood screws into each of the side, front, and back pieces into the bottom piece edges.

3. With the box fully assembled, cut the top portion using a table saw. Set the guide at a width of 2". Place the box on its front side and cut along the front, reposition the box on its end, and cut along the side; repeat for the rear, and the other end.

4. Attach the piano hinge to the top piece and then attach it to the top using the small wood screws provided with the hinge.

5. Attach the hasp to the center front underside of the top piece and fit the catch to the hasp and install it to the front piece.

6. Fit the chain to the box and top so that the lid falls back slightly. See finished view.

7. Attach a handle on each side of the box using wood screws

**Make the removable top tray.**

1. Cut pieces (E), (F), (G), and (H) as shown in the cutting list, using a table saw.

2. Attach the tray front/back (G) to the tray bottom (E) using wood glue and 6d finish nails.

3. Attach the tray sides (F) to the tray bottom (E) using wood glue and 6d finish nails.

4. Attach the tray handle (H) to the middle of the tray front/back using wood glue and 6d finish nails.

5. Measure down approximately 3" along the inside faces of the top of the box and mark a pencil line on the sides and front and back pieces.

6. Attach the tray supports to the inside of the box using wood glue and 4d finish nails.

7. Place the removable top tray inside the box.

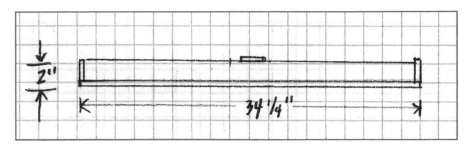

Figure 3 - Tray

## APPLY FINISHING TOUCHES

1. Fill all visible holes with wood putty.

2. Sand the entire surface using a sander.

3. Paint the outer surface using exterior-grade paint. Hunter green was used for this project. Paint a camouflage pattern using brown and black paint. Apply at least two coats. The interior surfaces were left unfinished.

4. Cut two pieces of 2" foam approximately 11 1/2" long. Using silicone RTV, glue the pieces inside the top door. Place them 8" from each end. Cut five or six slices about 1" deep, evenly spaced across the foam. Store your arrows within these cut slots.

Not only can this shelf hold framed photos, but it can also hold knickknacks in your hunting den or library.

# 14

# BOWHUNTER'S PHOTO SHELF

---

### TOOLS

Table saw

Drill

Power miter box or hand miter box

Router

1/2" Provincial router bit

1/4" shank 25/64" keyhole bit

---

Deceptively simple to build, this elegant shelf mimics the look of hardwood at a fraction of the cost. It will receive praise from friends and family. It's a great place to display your favorite photos of memories of successful days afield with your bow.

You can also store little knickknacks, antique arrowheads, or small decorative pieces on a wall anywhere in the house.

Stock molding, miter cuts, and countersunk nails hide a support framework. An antique white paint finish disguises the shelf's inexpensive poplar lumber. You can replace the wood with pine if you are looking for a stained finish. It can be made larger by extending the length and width of shown dimensions.

Dimensions: 5 1/4" high; 4 1/2" deep; 18" long

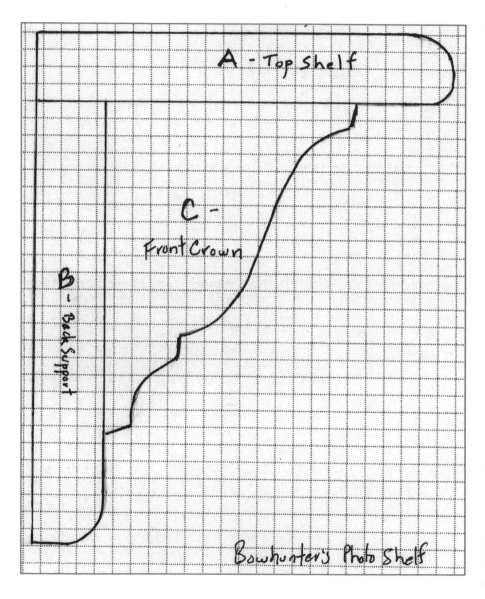

A - Top Shelf

C -
Front Crown

B - Back Support

Bowhunter's Photo Shelf

Figure 1 - Side View

116

## CUTTING LIST

| Key | Part | Dimensions | Pcs. | Material |
|-----|------|------------|------|----------|
| A | Top shelf | 3/4" x 4 1/2" x 18" | 1 | Poplar |
| B | Back support | 3/4" x 4 1/2" x 10 1/4" | 1 | Poplar |
| C | Front crown | 3-4" x 15 3/4" crown | 1 | Poplar |
| D | Side crown | 3-4" x 3 1/2" | 1 | Poplar |

**Materials**: Wood glue; finish nails (3/4", 2d, 4d), finishing materials such as white enamel paint.

Note: Measurements reflect the actual thickness of dimension lumber.

**Directions**:

Cut, shape, and assemble the top shelf (A), the back support (B).

1. Cut the top shelf (A) and back support (B) to size as shown in the cutting list.

2. Round off the top front and side edges of top shelf (A) using a 1/4" round router bit.

3. Round off the bottom front and side edges of the top shelf (A) using a 1/2" Provincial router bit.

4. Round off the bottom portion of the back support (B) using a 1/4" round router bit.

5. Center the back support (B) an equal distance from both ends of the top shelf (A). Drill three pilot holes through the top of the top shelf along the back edge. Use wood glue and 4d finish nails and attach the top shelf to the back support. Set the nail heads.

**Cut and attach the crown molding.**

1. Cut the front crown (C) and the side crown (D) to size. Miter the ends at 45 degrees by positioning the molding upside down in a power miter box, with one flat lip against the base of the saw, and the other lip against the saw fence.

2. Position the front crown so the top edge is flush with the bottom of the top shelf and so that the lower mitered ends match up to the bottom of the back support ends. Drill pilot holes along the

bottom of the crown molding and attach the front crown to the back support using wood glue and 3/4" finish nails. Drill a few more pilot holes on the top potion of the crown molding and nail it to the bottom of the top shelf.

3. Attach the side crowns in the same way. Lock-nail (see note) the crown molding joints with 2d finish nails. Set all nail heads. (Author's note: Lock-nailing is a technique used to reinforce mitered joints. The idea is to drive finish nails through both mating surfaces at the joint. Start by drilling pilot holes all the way through one board— this avoids splitting the wood—and partway into the other mating surface. Drive a small finish nail, such as a 2d or 4d or a brad, through each pilot hole to complete the lock-nailing procedure.)

**Mount the shelf.**

1. Prior to mounting the shelf to a wall, holes need to be made in the back of the back support. Drill two 1/4" holes 1/4" deep at two locations in the back of the back support approximately 2 1/2" from side and bottom edges. Use a 25/64" keyhole bit on the router and go up 1" toward the top of back support.

2. The shelf can be mounted anywhere on a wall. Use anchors if there are no studs in the area, line up the back holes, and install anchors. Use wood screws and slip the shelf back over the screw heads and push down. Use a level when placing the anchors or screws into the wall.

## APPLY FINISHING TOUCHES

1. Remove the shelf from the wall and apply putty to all nail holes. Scrape off excess glue.

2. Finish-sand the shelf, apply the finish, and allow drying time. Apply at least two coats after priming. Use smooth sand paper or steel wool on final coat. (Author's note: This shelf can be shortened or lengthened to meet your needs. To resize, simply adjust the sizes of the top shelf, back support, and moldings accordingly.)

# 15

# ARCHER'S BOOKCASE

## TOOLS

Table saw, circular saw, or hand saw

Hammer

Router with a 1/4" rabbet bit, 1/4" dado bit

T-square

Nail set

Palm sander or belt sander

Wood plane

I have built many bookcases over the past 25 years. Some are stand-alone cases that can be placed anywhere depending on your room layout. Others have been built-in wall units, permanently attached, made to fit in corners, between sectional walls, or around fireplaces or windows. Obviously, all have been made to display collection of books.

This bookshelf is different; it is not only for display of your books, but also for the storage of your bow accessories including a few of your bows. Doors have been installed on the bottom portion of the bookcase, for storage of your various archery supplies. A lock was used for added security to keep the youngsters from getting at any sharp objects such as your broadheads or hunting knives.

As you can see from the photo, a 3" Shaker peg has been installed on both sides for a convenient place to hangs your bows, one on each side. Hence, our name the archer's bookcase.

This design is considered a "tall" bookcase, but can be modified to any height you desire. It can be made taller, shorter, and wider, with more or fewer shelves, and shelf spacing can be varied. The shelves were made to be fixed in place, but can be modified so some of them are adjustable.

Poplar was used since we painted the unit, with a semi-gloss latex hunter green color. Arrows were made using dowels and wooden shapes for broadheads and vanes. If you intend to stain and finish with a clear coat of varnish or polyurethane, use pine as the least expensive wood. For a more upgraded bookcase, other woods can be used such as oak or maple.

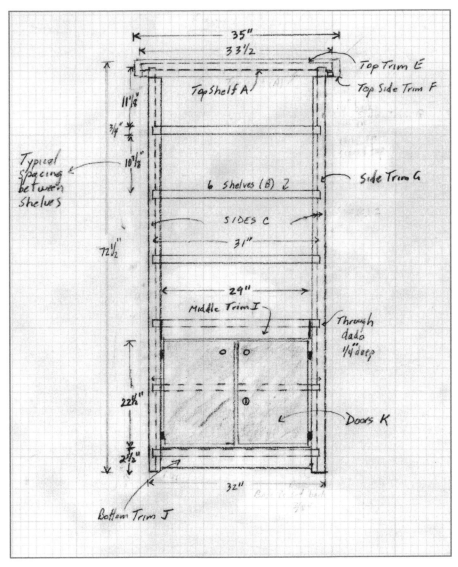

Figure 1 - Front View

Dimensions: 72 1/2" high; 10 3/4" deep; 33 1/2" wide

## CUTTING LIST

| Key | Part | Dimensions | Pcs. | Material |
|-----|------|-----------|------|----------|
| A | Top shelf | 3/4" x 10 3/4" x 33 1/2" | 1 | Poplar |
| B | Shelves | 3/4" x 10 1/2" x 31" | 6 | Poplar |
| C | Sides | 3/4" x 10 3/4" x 72" | 2 | Poplar |
| D | Back | 1/4" x 30 3/4" x 72" | 1 | Poplar |
| E | Top Trim | 3/4" x 2 1/2" x 35" | 1 | Poplar |
| F | Top side trim | 3/4" x 1 1/2" x 10 3/4" | 2 | Poplar |
| G | Side trim | 3/4" x 1 1/2" x 71 1/4" | 2 | Poplar |
| H | Side filler pcs | 3/4" x 3/4" x 10 3/4" | 2 | Poplar |
| I | Middle Trim | 3/4" x 2 1/2" x 29" | 1 | Poplar |
| J | Bottom trim | 3/4" x 2 1/2" x 29" | 1 | Poplar |
| K | Doors | 3/4" x 14 3/8" x 22" | 2 | Poplar |
| | | | | Plywood |
| L | Arrow shafts | 1/4" x 25" | 2 | Birch |
| M | Arrow heads | 1/4" x 2 1/2" x 2' | 2 | Birch |
| N | Arrow vanes | 3/16" x 2 3/4" x 1 3/8" | 2 | Birch |

**Materials**: Wood glue; 4d and 6d finish nails; 1" brads; wood putty; four 2" x 1 1/2" brass hinges with screws; two knobs; two half-turn buttons, one 3/4" door utility lock; two Shaker pegs with screws, #10-7/8" x 3" long.

Note: Measurements reflect the actual thickness of dimension lumber. The arrowheads and the vanes can be made from 1/4" stock, or more simply, purchased at an arts and crafts store. They are also available at www.craftparts.com.

### Directions:
Measure and cut pieces (A), (B), (C), and (D) as shown in cutting list using a table saw or circular saw.

1. Using a block plane or palm sander, make sure all edges are smooth and square.

2. Cut the rabbet joints on the top (A) and side pieces (C) as described below. Use a router with a 3/4" dado bit and a side guide. Set the depth of the router bit at 1/4" deep.

    A. Lay out the top shelf on your workbench or on another flat surface. Set the side guide so that the bit will give you a dado joint at 3/4" from each end. Carefully run the router across the board at each end.

    B. Lay out the sides on your workbench or another flat surface side-by- side. Mark the locations of the dado cuts as shown in Figure 1, using a large T-square. Use a wood clamp at both ends to ensure that the two sides lie side-by-side. Use a straightedge piece of wood approximately 1/2" x 1" wide as a guide for the router. Using two small C-clamps at each side, secure the wood as a guide such that the router bit lines up in the desired location of the dado joint. Carefully run the router across the boards at the location. Repeat this same procedure for the remaining dado cuts along the side pieces.

## Assemble the shelves.

1. Lay out both side pieces (C) on end about 32" apart. Place a dab of wood glue in the dado joints. Be careful to use only a modest amount to avoid excess glue running out the sides onto the shelves.

2. Place all of the shelves (B) between the dado joints. Make sure that the front edges of the shelves are flush with the front edge of the side pieces. Using three 4d finish nails for each end and nail through the side board into the shelf ends. Repeat the same for the other side. Repeat for the remaining shelves.

3. Set the top shelf (A) on the top ends of the sides so that the back edge is flush with the back edge of the side pieces. Use some wood glue and three 4d finish nails and nail in from the top.

4. Lay the assembled bookcase on its front edge so that the rear edges are accessible. Using a router with a dado bit set at a depth of 1/4", run the router around the entire inside edge of the top and sides.

5. Apply some wood glue to the dado joints around the top and sides. Also place a line of glue on the rear shelf edges of each shelf. Position the back piece (D) between the dado joints and on the shelf edges. Using 1" brads, nail the back piece to the edges. Space the brads about 8" apart along the dado e dges and along the back of each shelf.

**Install trim and doors.**

1. Install the top side trim piece (F) on the end of the top shelf (A). It should overhang the top by 1/4". Use 6d finish nails and wood glue to nail in the end of the top shelf. Place the side filler piece (H) between the side shelf and the top side trim (F) and secure in place using wood glue and 6d finish nails. Repeat for the other side.

2. Install the top trim (E) on the front edge of the top shelf (A) by using wood glue and 6d nails.

3. Install the side trim (G) along the front edge of the side (C). Ensure that it is flush with the outside side edge. Use wood glue and 6d finish nails. Repeat for the other side.

4. Install the middle trim (I) so it lies flush with the top of the third shelf. Use wood glue and 6d nails.

5. Install the bottom trim (J) so it lies flush with the top of the bottom shelf. Use wood glue and 6d nails.

6. Install the doors by using two hinges on each side. Mount two hinges on the door so that one is 1 1/2" from the top and the other is 1 1/2" from the bottom. Place the door on one side, position it so that there is an equal space in the opening, and mount the hinges to the side trim. Repeat for the other door.

7. Drill a 1/16" hole for the knobs and install one on each door.

8. Install two half-turn buttons on the inside of the left-side door, one on the bottom and the other on the top of the door.

9. Install the cabinet lock on the other door. Drill a 3/4" hole, approximately 3/4" from the edge, midway along the door edge.

## APPLY FINISHING TOUCHES

1. Install a Shaker peg on each side of the shelf unit for a handy place to hang your bows. The ones shown on page 119 were

placed in the middle of the shelf, 10" down from the top. However, they can be placed in any location you desire.

2. Using wood glue, attach an arrow shaft (L) on the front surface of the top trim (E) centered between the two side trim pieces (G).

3. Using wood glue, attach an arrowhead (M) on one end of the shaft.

4. If the arrow vane-shaped pieces (N) were purchased at an arts and crafts store or online, cut approximately 1/4" off the triangular end. Using wood glue, attach an arrow vane (N) on the other end of the shaft.

5. Repeat Steps 2-4 for the middle trim (I).

6. Set all the finish nails with a nail set.

7. Fill all visible holes with wood putty.

8. Sand the entire surface using a sander.

9. Stain, lacquer, varnish, or paint the bookcase as desired.

Here's a closer shot of the doors, knobs, and lock. It's always a good idea to install a lock on a case like this, especially if you store broadheads or ammunition in it.

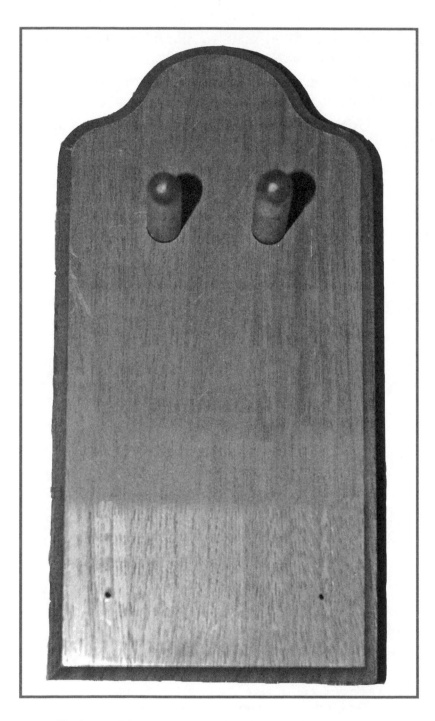

The bow rack is easy to make and can be hung almost anywhere.

# 16

# WALL-HANGING
# BOW RACK

How often have you come back from bowhunting to the deer camp or even your home and had to struggle to find a place to hang your bow on the porch, in the garage, or even inside the house or camp? If you're like me, finding a place to hang a bow safely and conveniently has proven to be both frustrating and difficult.

Many times I have gotten so annoyed looking for a place to put my bow out of harm's way between the morning and evening hunts that I wound up either putting it on my bed at deer camp or back in the bow case at home. Of course, that meant also taking my arrows out of the quiver and storing them separately as well.

When we bought our farm, we hung storage hooks on the back deck, and when we returned from a hunt we hung the bows from the hooks. While this worked, it always left the bows exposed to the elements. One day it was so windy that the bows swung from side to side as they hung there.

Leo stared at them as they drifted back and forth in the breeze. I could smell the odor of wood burning, as he concentrated on a solution to the problem at hand. Moments later he announced, "I've got it; I know what to build to solve this problem!" Without another word he was off to the shop. About two hours later we were hanging our unfinished "bow-holders" all over the place.

Some hung on the deck for use in calm weather, and some hung in the trophy room of our deer camp. That was several years ago and ever since we have never had to worry about where to place our bows when we return from a hunt.

The Wall-Hanging Bow Rack has become part of our bowhunting equipment. I even take one with me when I'm going bowhunting to tape an episode for our television show *Woods 'N Water,* which is seen on The Sportsman Channel (visit our Web site for exact times and dates of our show, at www.woodsnwater.tv). I can hang it in my room or in a safe place out of the wind outside on the deck.

Keeping your bow safe from someone accidentally bumping into it, moving it, or just handling it, is paramount to keeping everything—especially your sights and rests—from being moved or broken.

The best parts about building this handy bow rack are that it is very simple to make, it can be hung anywhere without taking up much room, and once finished it looks nice as well. A tip from Leo is to make several of them so you'll have some extras for guests and to hang in different places for yourself as well. The one in the book is made from solid oak and finished with a stain and then protected with a varnish finish. Any type of wood will work just as well, however.

Dimensions: 7" high; 3 1/2" wide

## CUTTING LIST

| Key | Part | Dimensions | Pcs. | Material |
|-----|------|------------|------|----------|
| A | Wall rack | 3/4" x 3 1/2" x 7" | 1 | Oak |
| B | Dowels | 1/4" x 2 3/4" | 1 | Oak |

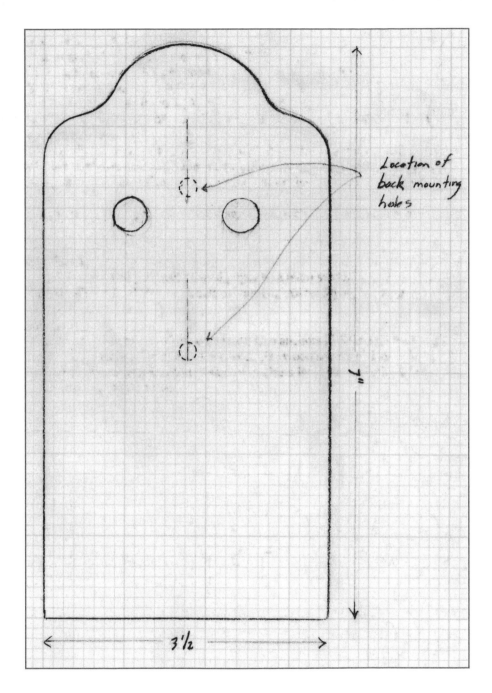

Location of back mounting holes

7"

3½

Figure 1 - Front View

**Materials:** Wood glue

Note: Measurements reflect the actual thickness of dimension lumber.

**Directions:**

Cut and shape the wall rack (A).

1. Cut the wall rack (A) to size as shown in Figure 1.

2. Finish off the front edge with a router using a 1/4" round router bit.

3. Drill 1/4" holes as shown through to the back.

4. Round off the tips of both dowels (B) by sanding the ends.

5. Place a little glue in the hole and tap the dowels into the hole so that the dowels lie even with the back.

6. Prior to mounting, holes need to be made in the back of the wall rack. Drill two 1/4" holes 1/4" deep at two locations in the back of the wall rack, approximately 2 1/2" apart along the center line of the rack. Use a keyhole bit on the router and go up 1" toward the top of each hole.

7. Cut a piece of green felt the same shape as the rack and glue it to the back.


**APPLY FINISHING TOUCHES**

1. Finish-sand the rack using a sheet of sandpaper or a palm sander.

2. Apply a coat of stain, and then two coats of varnish. Allow drying time between coats.


**MOUNT THE WALL RACK**

The wall rack can be mounted anywhere. Use anchors if there are no studs in the area, line up the back holes and install anchors. Use wood screws and slip the shelf back over the screw heads and push down. Use a level when placing the anchors or screws into the wall.

# 17

# ARCHER'S
# BOW AND ARROW RACK

## TOOLS

Hand saw and miter box or table saw

Hammer

Router

1/4" round over router bit

Drill and 3/16", 1/16" bits

Palm sander

Screw gun

Square

Jigsaw

This rack not only creates a sturdy, organized bow storage area, it also makes a great addition to your trophy room. We all know how much money we spend on archery equipment, so why not display your favorite bow and arrows? This design accommodates two different bows and up to 12 arrows. It has a lower shelf for storage of small bow accessories such as spare strings, broadheads, target tips, nocks, and other miscellaneous items. A hinged door was added to conceal these items. Although this design does not have one, a lock can be installed for additional security. Solid oak was used; stain was applied and finished with satin polyurethane.

Dimensions: 26" long; 28" wide; 4" deep

## CUTTING LIST

| Key | Part | Dimensions | Pcs. | Material |
|-----|------|------------|------|----------|
| A | Bottom plate | 3/4" x 4" x 25" | 1 | Red oak |
| B | Bottom Arrow plate | 3/4" x 4" x 25" | 1 | Red oak |
| C | Top Arrow plate | 3/4" x 4" x 25" | 1 | Red oak |
| D | Top plate | 3/4" x 4" x 25" | 1 | Red oak |
| E | Side plates | 3/4" x 4" x 28" | 2 | Red oak |

| Key | Part | Dimensions | Pcs. | Material |
|-----|------|-----------|------|----------|
| F | Door | 3/4" x 4" x 26 1/2" | 1 | Red oak |
| G | Back | 1/2" x 3 1/2" x 25" | 1 | Plywood |

**Materials:** Wood glue; 1 1/4" wood screws; 1" brads; polyurethanc; lacquer and/or stain; 14 - 1/4" oak buttons; piano hinge 1/2" x 25"; brass knob; two door latches; four Shaker pegs with screws, #10- 7/8" x 3" long.

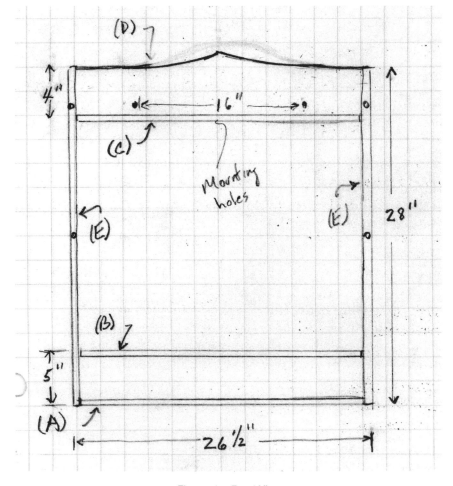

Figure 1 - Front View

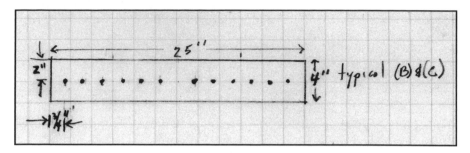

Figure 2 - Top View Arrow Plate

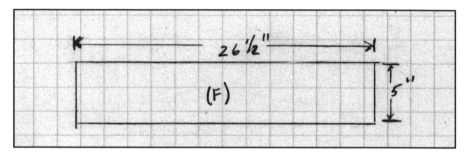

Figure 3 - Door

Note: Measurements reflect the actual thickness of dimension lumber.

Measure and cut all the pieces (A), (B), (C), (D), (E), and (F) as shown in cutting list. Use a hand saw and miter box or table saw to get square cuts.

**Directions:**

**Assemble the frame.**

1. Lay out one of the side plates (E) on a flat surface. Measure and mark the locations of seven holes, as shown in Figure 4. Using a 3/16" bit, drill pilot holes through the plate. Repeat this for the other plate (E).

2. Using a jigsaw, round off the front top corner of each side plate (E), as shown in Figure 4.

3. Lay out both side plates (E) on end, spaced approximately 25" apart. Place the bottom plate (A), the bottom arrow plate (B), and the top arrow plate (C) between the side plates (E) at the locations, as shown in Figure 1.

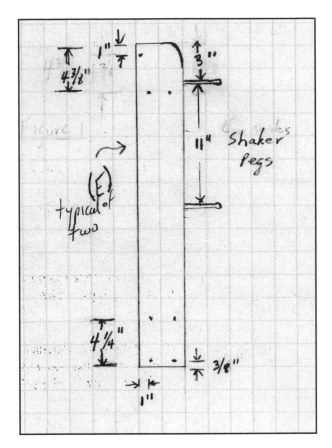

Figure 4 - Side View

4. Put a dab of wood glue at each end of the plates. Using two wood screws and a screw gun, secure each plate to the side plate. Repeat for the other side.

5. Using a jigsaw, cut the shape of the top plate (D). This shape can be cut as shown or changed to meet your needs.

6. Place the top plate (D) in its proper location, as shown in Figure 1. Use wood glue along the ends and along the bottom edges. Screw in place using a wood screw at each end. Drill three 3/16" pilot holes equidistant on the bottom side of the top arrow plate (C), 3/16" from the back edge. Using three wood screws and a screw gun, secure the top arrow plate to the top plate.

7. Use a square to make sure that the frame assembly is squared up.

8. Place the back (G) in place behind the door and secure by nailing a few 1" brads along the bottom plate (A) and the bottom arrow plate (B). You might want to pre-drill the holes.

## APPLY FINISHING TOUCHES

1. Mark the locations of the arrow holes in the top arrow plate (C) and bottom arrow plate (B), as shown in Figure 2.

2. Using a drill and 1/4" bit, drill 12 holes through the top arrow plate. Drill holes only 1/2" deep in the top of the bottom arrow plate.

3. Using a router with a 1/4" ogee bit, finish off the following edges: along the outside edge of the side plates (E), along the top edge of the top plate (D), along the bottom front edge of the top arrow plate (C), and around the outside front edges of the door (F).

4. Using a piano hinge, mount the door (F) to the bottom plate (A).

5. Mount two cabinet latches on both sides inside the door enclosure.

6. Drill a 1/8" hole in the center, at 1" from the top edge of the door, and install a knob.

7. Place the oak plugs in each of the seven holes on each side plate. Use a small amount of wood glue, and tap in place using a hammer.

8. Install four Shaker pegs on the front edge of the side plate, two on each side at the locations shown in Figure 4. Pre-drill holes using a 1/16" bit.

9. Finish-sand the surfaces of the rack. Stain, lacquer, shellac, or varnish the rack as desired.

10. The rack's location and the type of wall surface will determine the mounting of the rack. If mounting on standard frame wall, two 1/4" holes can be drilled at 16" center and then secured to the wall using 2-3" panhead brass wood screws (see Figure 1).

# 18

# PAPER TUNING STAND

This is a simple-to-make paper target holder for tuning the flight of your arrows. Note the sand bag at the base. I put hay bales behind the target to stop arrows.

## TOOLS

PVC hand saw

Miter box

Are your arrows not flying true? Do they wobble in flight? If so, it's time for you to make this simple project. It gives clues to changes that should be made to give you perfect or near perfect arrow flight.

It is made of standard PVC pipe and fittings available at your local plumbing supply store or a major store, such as Home Depot or Lowe's. Once the tuning stand is built, simply tape a piece of white paper to the top and middle rails. It is important that the paper is taunt within the stand. The stand is light and portable. The height of the stand ensures that the paper is high enough so its center is even with the height of the arrow as it is fired from the bow, using good shooting form. A good backstop is placed 4 or 5 feet behind the paper so the arrow passes completely through the paper before it hits the backstop. This will assure that the tears in the paper caused by the arrow passing through will not be affected by how the arrow moves when it hits the backstop.

Dimensions: 67" high; 32" wide

## CUTTING LIST

| Key | Part | Dimensions | Pcs. | Material |
|-----|------|-----------|------|----------|
| A | Base long supports | 1 1/2" x 28" | 2 | PVC |
| B | Base short supports | 1 1/2" x 13" | 4 | PVC |
| C | Short uprights | 1 1/2" x 25" | 2 | PVC |
| D | Long uprights | 1 1/2" x 36" | 2 | PVC |
| E | Middle upright | 1 1/2" x 28" | 1 | PVC |
| F | Top upright | 1 1/2" x 28" | 1 | PVC |

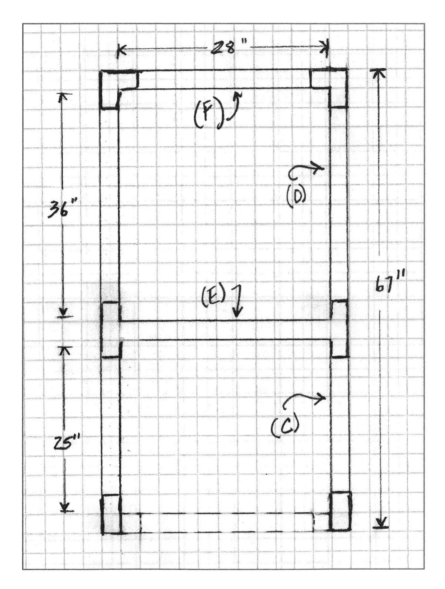

Figure 1 - Front View

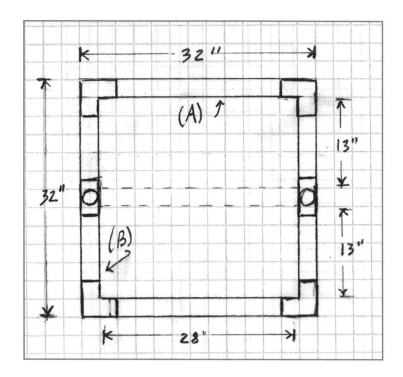

Figure 2 - Top View

**Materials:** PVC cement, assorted PVC fittings as follows: six 1 1/2" 90-degree elbows, four 1 1/2" Ts

**Directions:**

Cut all the PVC pieces (A), (B), (C), (D), (E), and (F) to the specified lengths as shown in the cutting list using a PVC hand saw and miter box.

**Assemble the paper tuning stand.**

1. Place the long base supports (A) on a flat surface approximately 32" apart.

2. Using PVC cement, attach a 1 1/2" 90-degree elbow at each end of (A). Make sure that the elbows lie flat. (Author's note: Unless otherwise stated, use PVC cement when attaching the remaining PVC pieces together.)

3. Attach short base supports (B) to the other side of each 90-degree elbow. Connect the base together by using a 1 1/2" T on each side. Make sure that the top of the T is facing in the vertical upright position.

4. Attach a short upright (C) in the T on each side.

5. Attach a 1 1/2" T to the top end of the short upright on each side. Make sure that the T faces inward.

6. Attach the middle upright in the ends of both Ts.

7. Attach a long upright (D) in the vertical end of the T on each side.

8. Attach a 90-degree elbow at the top of each long upright. Make sure that the elbows face inward.

9. Attach the top upright (F) into the other ends of both 90-degree elbows.

The paper tuning rack is ready to use. Simply tape a piece of white paper to the middle upright and the top upright, and you can begin to shoot through the rack to tune your arrows.

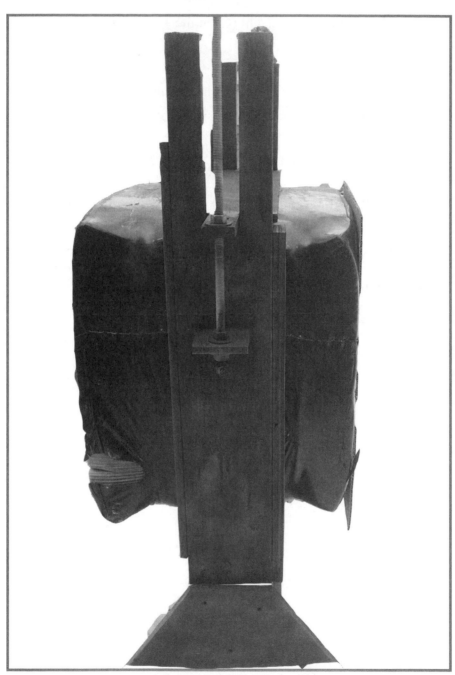

This side-view shot of the reusable practice target stand shows how the top bar gets tightened down on the foam target to secure it in place.

# 19

# BOWHUNTER'S REUSABLE PRACTICE TARGET

## TOOLS

Hand saw or table saw

Hammer

Drill and 3/8" wood bit and metal bit

Screw gun

Square

Jigsaw

3/8" wrench

Believe it or not, I saw this practice stand at a friend's house almost ten years ago. When I was asked to write this book, this is one of the first projects I thought of adding to the table of contents. The reasons were simple: this practice stand is so practical; it can easily be moved, and you can use cardboard, Styrofoam, or simply place a pre-made target block in it.

As mentioned above, I first saw this stand at a friend's house. I can't take credit for this design; only for providing the step-by-step directions for making one similar to his.

John Bennete deserves credit for the design. A retired carpenter, John spends much of his time bowhunting, mostly in eastern Long Island-poor unlucky guy. All kidding aside, I am sure he spends the off-season using this practice stand to keep in shape.

Dimensions: 46" high; 33" wide; 22" deep

## CUTTING LIST

| Key | Part | Dimensions | Pcs. | Material |
|-----|------|-----------|------|----------|
| A | Vertical Sides | 1 1/2" x 5 1/2" x 46" | 2 | ACQ |
| B | Shelf | 1 1/2" x 5 1/2" x 24" | 1 | ACQ |
| C | Bottom supports | 3/4" x 3 1/2" x 27" | 2 | ACQ plywood |
| D | Front stops | 3/4" x 3 1/2" x 22" | 2 | ACQ plywood |
| E | End supports | 3/4" x 12" x 22" | 2 | ACQ plywood |
| F | Shelf supports | 3/4" x 5 1/2" x 12" | 2 | ACQ plywood |

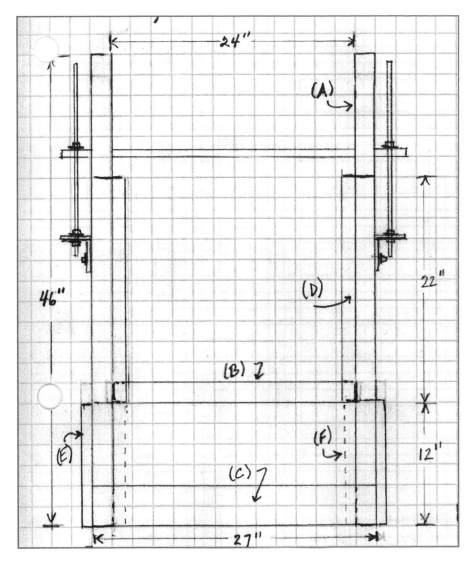

Figure 1 - Front View

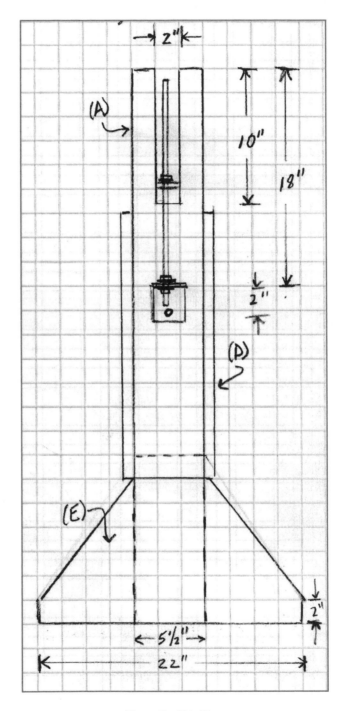

Figure 2 - Side View

146

**Materials:** Wood glue; 3" and 1 1/2" decking screws; 3/8" thick steel plate, 6" x 33"; two 3/8" galvanized threaded bolts 20" long, six 3/8" nuts and flat washers; two 3 x 3" L-brackets, 3" wide; two 3/8" x 3" carriage bolts, nuts, and washers.

Note: Measurements reflect the actual thickness of dimension lumber.

**Directions:**

Measure and cut all the pieces (A), (B), (C), (D), (E) and (F) as shown in cutting list. Use a hand saw, circular saw, or table saw.

    1. Using a hand saw, jigsaw, or table saw, make the cutout in pieces (A), as shown in Figure 2.

    2. Using a hand saw or jigsaw, cut the shape of pieces (E), as shown in Figure 2.

    3. Have the cutout made, as shown in Figure 3, for the metal top plate. We recommend that you have this done at a steel and iron shop, including the drilling of a 3/8" hole at each end of the plate.

**Assemble the frame.**

    1. Lay out the two vertical sides (A) on a flat surface approximately 24" apart. Place the shelf (B) 12" from the bottom. Secure in place by using wood glue and three 3" decking screws into the ends on each side.

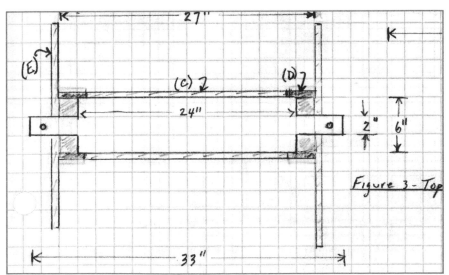

Figure 3 - Top View

2. Place the bottom supports (C) at the bottom of the vertical sides (A). Secure in place by using wood glue and two 1 1/2" decking screws at each of the four locations.

3. Place the end supports (E) on both sides and secure in place by using wood glue and five 1 1/2" decking screws.

4. Place the bottom shelf supports (F) under each shelf against the vertical sides. Secure in place using wood glue and six 1 1/2" decking screws on each side.

5. Place the front stops (D) against the front edge of the vertical sides (A). Secure in place using wood glue and six 1 1/2" decking screws on each side.

6. Using a drill and a 3/8" metal bit, drill two holes in the 3" x 3" brackets. One hole should be drilled in the middle of the top of the bracket, and the other in the middle of the bottom side of the bracket.

7. Using a drill with a 3/8" wood bit, drill a hole in the center of each vertical side (A), 20" down from the top (see Figure 2).

8. Mount the bracket on each side using a carriage bolt, nut, and washer. Tighten using a 3/8" open-end wrench.

9. Place a threaded rod in each of the brackets. Secure in place using a nut and washer on each side of the bracket, as shown in Figure 1.

10. Place the metal top plate in the cutout of the vertical sides so that the ends of the plate fit over the top ends of the threaded rods.

**Place the desired target material in the target.** The design of this target allows you to use layers of cardboard, Styrofoam, or a target block between the metal top plate and the bottom shelf. Cardboard is good if you're shooting target tips; Styrofoam works well if using broadheads, and either target tips or broadheads may work, depending on the type of target block used.

1. If you are using cardboard, cut the pieces so they fit between the two vertical sides. Make the cardboard at least 24" deep.

2. Layer the cardboard so that it fills in the space from the bottom shelf and the top metal plate. Using enough cardboard pieces,

make sure that the top metal plate sits a few inches higher than the bottom cutout in the vertical sides.

3. Using a 3/8" wrench, tighten down the nuts on both sides evenly until the cardboard is crushed as tightly as possible. The target is now ready to use. As you shoot arrows into the target, periodically tighten the nuts to keep the cardboard as tight as possible.

4. Repeat this same procedure using dense Styrofoam.

5. If neither cardboard nor Styrofoam is used, simply get a block target slightly smaller than the opening of this stand. Place it on the bottom shelf and tighten up on the nuts.

# 20

# PRACTICE ARROW
# HOLDER

**TOOLS**

Drill and 1/8" drill bit
PVC hand saw

This is one of the simpler projects and yet very practical for those of us who practice around the house. It is so simple we did not think it was necessary to provide the drawings. It is made of standard PVC pipe and fittings. It holds both broadheads and target tip arrows. A handle made from a wire clothes hanger makes the holder easy to handle. It also makes it easy to store the holder on a hook in your garage or archer's shed when not in use.

This project is so easy, inexpensive, and practical that we have made more than a dozen of them. We have placed them throughout some of our trails on our farm, 20–30 yards away from various 3-D targets.

Dimensions: 24" high; 4" wide

## CUTTING LIST

| Key | Part | Dimensions | Pcs. | Material |
|-----|------|-----------|------|----------|
| A | Arrow holder | 3"x 24–36" | 1 | PVC |
| B | Bottom flange | 3" Toilet flange | 1 | PVC |

**Materials:** 12" piece of wire hanger; brown, black, and green spray paint; PVC cement, small piece of foam, about 3" diameter.

## Directions:

1. Cut the desired length of 3-inch PVC pipe. For short arrows, 24" is recommended. Make this longer depending on the length of your arrows.

2. Place the toilet flange on a flat surface. Using PVC cement on the bottom of the cut pipe and on the inside of the toilet flange, place the pipe in the flange, twisting it slightly until flush with the bottom. Allow to dry for ten minutes.

3. Drill a 1/8" hole on each side of the top of the PVC pipe at locations, as shown in Figure 1.

4. Bend the piece of wire hanger to shape, as shown in Figure 2 and then place it in each of the holes.

5. Using black, brown, and green spray paint, spray the bow and arrow holder, making a camouflage pattern. Wait at least 30 minutes between colors.

Place the small piece of foam in the bottom of the arrow holder to provide protection for the arrow tips.

# 21

# BOW AND ARROW
# PRACTICE STAND

---

**TOOLS**

Drill and 1/8" drill bit

PVC hand saw

Miter box

Needlenose pliers

---

We built the archer's shed, the archer's target stand, and then found that something was missing. Since the shed and target are out in an open field, there is no place to hang our bows or store our arrows when target shooting. I can't tell you how many times, when laying my bow on the ground to retrieve my arrows from the target, that someone came quite close to stepping on my bow. Therefore, the need for a freestanding bow and arrow practice stand was born.

Another relatively easy project to make is this bow and arrow practice stand. It is made of standard PVC pipe and fittings. It holds a couple of bows and provides a convenient place to store practice arrows while target shooting. Both broadheads and target tip arrows can be stored. It is portable so place it anywhere you want, set up your target, and you are ready to go.

Dimensions: 65" high; 19" wide

---

## CUTTING LIST

| Key | Part | Dimensions | Pcs. | Material |
|-----|------|-----------|------|----------|
| A | Toilet flange | 3" toilet flange | 1 | PVC |
| B | Nipple | 3" | 1 | PVC |
| D | Arrow holder | 3" x 12" | 1 | PVC |
| E | Nipples | 2" x 2" long | 2 | PVC |
| G | Support pipe | 1 1/2" x 8-10" long | 1 | PVC |
| J | Bow support | 1 1/2" x 30" long | 1 | PVC |
| M | Bow holder 1 | 1 1/2" x 2" long | 1 | PVC |
| N | Nipple | 1 1/2" x 3" long | 1 | PVC |

---

| Key | Part | Dimensions | Pcs. | Material |
|-----|------|------------|------|----------|
| P | Nipple | 1 1/2" x 2" long | 1 | PVC |
| Q | Bow holder 2 | 1 1/2" x 5" long | 1 | PVC |
| R | Bottom plate | 3/4" x 12" x 20" | 1 | Exterior-grade plywood |

**Materials:** 12" piece of wire hanger; brown, black, and green spray paint; PVC cement and assorted PVC fittings as follows: one 3" x 2" reducing Y (part C); one 2" x 1 1/2" reducing coupling (part H); two 1 1/2" straight 45-degree elbows (parts I and L); one 1 1/2" T-fitting part K); one 2" x 1 1/2" Y (parts F and O), three 1 1/2" plugs; three 3/4" long # 6 wood screws; small piece of foam about 3"diameter.

### Directions:

Cut all the PVC nipples and other pieces (B through Q) to the specified lengths, as shown in the cutting list, using a PVC hand saw and miter box.

#### Assemble the arrow holder and base.

1. Place the toilet flange (A) on a flat surface. Using PVC cement on the bottom of the cut pipe and on the inside of the toilet flange, place the nipple (B) in the flange, twisting it slightly until flush with the bottom. Allow cement to dry for a few minutes.

2. Using PVC cement, place the 3" x 2" Y (C) on top of (B). Make sure that the Y is facing up.

3. Attach (D) into the top of (C).

4. Drill an 1/8" hole on each side at the top of PVC pipe (D) approximately 1" from the top.

5. Bend the piece of wire hanger to shape, as shown in Figure 1, and then place it in each of the holes. Using a pair of needlenose pliers, bend the tips of the wire on both sides inside of the pipe.

6. Screw down the toilet flange using 3/4" #6 wood screws to the bottom wood plate (R), as shown in Figure 1.

#### Assemble the bow holder.

1. Attach the nipple (E) into the Y portion of (C).

155

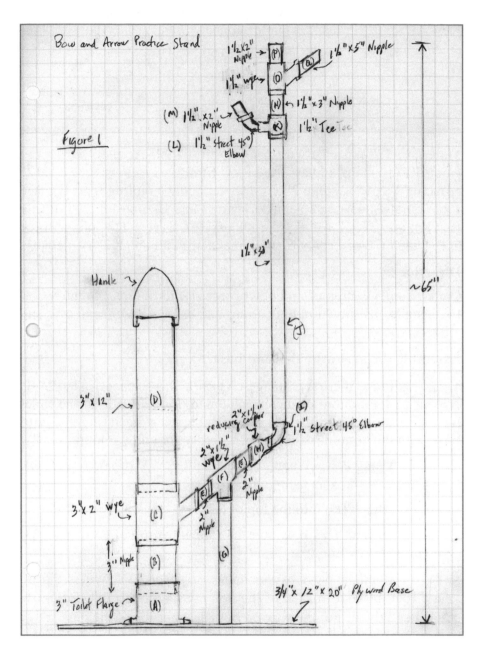

Bow and Arrow Practice Stand

Figure 1

Handle

1½"x2" Nipple (P)

1½" wye (O)

1½"x5" Nipple (Q)

1½"x3" Nipple (N)

(M) 1½"x2" Nipple

1½" Tee Tee (K)

(L) 1½" Street 45° Elbow

1½"x3"

(J)

3"x12" (D)

2"x1½" reducing coupler

1½" Street 45° Elbow (I)

(H)

2"x1½" wye (E)

2" Nipple (E)

(F)

2" Nipple

3"x2" wye (C)

(G)

2" Nipple (E)

3" Nipple (B)

3" Toilet Flange (A)

3/4"x12"x20" Plywood Base

~65"

Figure 1 - Side View

156

2. Attach the 2" x 1 1/2" Y (F) into the other end of (E). Make sure that the bottom of the Y faces the bottom plate.

3. Attach another nipple (E) into the top portion of the Y (F).

4. Attach the 2" x 1 1/2" reducing coupling to (E).

5. Attach the 1 1/2" straight 45-degree elbow (I) into (H). Make sure that the top of the elbow faces up in a vertical position and is parallel to the arrow holder section.

6. Attach the bow support (J) into (I).

7. Attach the 1 1/2" T (K) onto (J).

8. Attach the 1 1/2" straight 45-degree elbow (L) into the side of the T (K). Make sure that the elbow is lined up in the vertical upright position.

9. Attach the bow holder 1 (M) into (L).

10. Attach the nipple (N) into top of (K).

11. Attach the 1 1/2" Y (O) into the top of (N). Make sure that the Y faces up and it is faced 180 degrees from the bottom bow holder (M).

12. Attach the nipple (P) into the top of (O).

13. Attach the bow holder 2 (Q) into (O).

14. Attach 1 1/2" plugs into the top pipe sections at locations (M), (P), and (Q).

## APPLY FINISHING TOUCHES

1. Using three different colors (black, brown, and green) spray paint the bow and arrow holder, creating a camouflage pattern. Wait at least 30 minutes between colors.

2. Place the small piece or foam in the bottom of the arrow holder to provide protection for the arrow tips.

Archer's equipment trailer; take a spare tire wherever you go.

# 22

# ARCHER'S EQUIPMENT TRAILER

This view of the trailer shows a mounted spare tire on the front. Even if you are only using the trailer around the farm, you should have a spare tire. If you are going to trailer heavier things, like an ATV, you may want to mount a trailer jack on the front so that it is easier to connect and disconnect to the hitch ball.

**TOOLS**

Table saw

Drill

Router

Ratchet set

After obtaining a standard 4' x 8' flatbed, single-axle trailer, you will want to make this handy trailer cargo rack. I purchased this used one for less than $100, scraped off the rust, coated the bottom steel with bottom coat spray tar, and spray-painted the outside steel rail supports with Rust-Oleum black paint. Total cost of the cargo rack including the undercoat, paint, wood, hardware, and lights was about $130.00.

This trailer is designed to ensure that what you put inside stays inside. We hook this trailer up to our RTV when setting up our portable tree stands in preparation for the bowhunting season. After our post-season and pre-season scouting is done, we decide on the locations of our portable stands, load them up in this trailer, and spend a day just transporting and setting the stands up. The trailer is small enough to navigate through our trails, yet large enough to carry anywhere from 8 to 16 stands. We do the same at the end of the season when we take the stands down to clean them up, paint them, and store them out of the weather for the following season.

The trailer with the railing is also useful to allow you to transport mulch and topsoil, which you can get for free from most local land-fills. I also use it to transport my deer carcasses to avoid messing up my SUV. If your trailer is smaller or larger, modify the dimensions accordingly to fit your trailer. If you plan to use this trailer to transport your leaves and brush, you can modify the height of the side railing by simply lengthening the uprights and adding the appropriate pieces of side railing. Depending on the rated weight capacity of the trailer springs, you could use this trailer to transport small tractor lawnmowers, other garden equipment, and your ATV.

Dimensions: 13" high; 4' wide; 8' long

## CUTTING LIST

| Key | Part | Dimensions | Pcs. | Material |
|-----|------|------------|------|----------|
| A | Uprights | 2" x 4" x 19" | 8 | Treated lumber |
| B | Back and front rails | 5/4" x 6" x 46" | 4 | Treated lumber |
| C | Side rails | 5/4" x 6' x 8' | 4 | Treated lumber |

**Materials:** 1/4" x 20" x 1 1/4" galvanized or stainless steel carriage bolts, washers, lock washers, and nuts; 1 1/2" wood deck screws; 1" x 12" wood screws and washers; trailer spare tire bracket; four sets of galvanized steel trailer brackets.

Note: Measurements reflect the actual thickness of dimension lumber.

**Directions:**

1. Cut eight pieces, uprights (A) at length of 19".

2. Cut four pieces, back and front rails (B) at 46" length.

3. Cut four pieces, side rails (C) at 8' length.

4. Construct the side railing.

    A. Place two uprights into side bracket supports, with about 14" above the bottom decking.

    B. Place one of the side rails on top deck, against the two uprights. Square the uprights and secure the side rail using 1 1/2" wood screws into the 2x4 uprights. Use four screws in each end of the side rail.

    C. Place the second side rail, using a space of about 1" between side rails and secure in same manner. Repeat for the other side.

5. Construct the back and front side railing.

    A. Place two uprights in the rear upright bracket supports, with about 14" above the bottom decking.

    B. Place one of the back rails on top of deck, against the two uprights. Make sure that the rail is placed between the ends of the side railing. Square the uprights and secure the rail using 1 1/2" wood screws into the 2x4 uprights. Use four screws in each end of rear rail.

C. Place the second back rail, using a space of about 1" between side rails and secure in same manner. Repeat for the front end.

6. Install the trailer brackets. These will allow you to easily remove the back railing.

A. Using one set (marked left and right), place the bracket on the middle of the top side rail and drill 1/4" holes through the holes in the bracket through the side rail. Mount the bracket using the 1/4" screws through the bracket, washers, lock washer, and nuts on the inside. Install the other one in the back rail, making sure that the back bracket lies into the bottom of the side bracket drilling holes and bolts in same manner.

B. Repeat for the other side.

C. Repeat Steps A and B for the front rail if you also want to be able remove the front railing. If not, use standard 1/2" 4x4 brackets, and bolt in the same manner.

7. You may apply an exterior-grade stain to the treated lumber or leave it unfinished, as it is made to withstand the elements.

Inside view of how the brackets are attached to the ends of the top rails.

8. Install trailer lights.

A. Mount the lights on the rear sides of the frame using L-brackets that are bolted to the back of lights, and then bolt the bracket into the side frame.

B. Run three-conductor, #14 exterior wire from both lights to the front of the trailer and connect to a trailer plug adapter. Secure the wire to the bottom supports using standard tie wraps. Use the appropriate plug for the type of outlet that is installed on your vehicle. Most likely, it will be a standard four-plug adapter. Check with your car parts supplier.

C. Plug into the vehicle plug with the vehicle lights on. Verify that the running lights work, the brake lights work, and the directionals work.

D. Ensure that a safety chain is installed and secure it to the trailer hitch whenever the trailer is in tow.

E. You are now ready to register your trailer. Complete the necessary forms depending on your local Department of Motor Vehicle laws.

9. Install spare tire bracket around frame of trailer front support. Install the tire so that two of the tire bolt holes align with the threaded ends, push tire in, and install the two tire support L pieces. A lock can be installed for security purposes.

Outside view of the brackets attached to the top rails.

The rock and rack jar is a nice addition to any room.

# 23

# ROCK AND RACK
# FLOWER JAR

**TOOLS**

Mixing pan, 6 x 10"

Scraper, 2–3"

Utility knife

This simple flower jar is a nice addition to the kitchen, den, or any other room in your camp in which you like to display flowers. The jar used in this project has a 2-inch opening on the top, a 7-inch base, and stands 12 inches high. Any other size or shape jar or vase could be used depending on your desire and need. It makes a great way to display your freshly cut flowers or synthetic flowers can be displayed in this jar.

The jar is covered with small stones and pieces of antlers from bow-harvested deer. After years of successful hunting, the racks begin to pile up, so why not make good use of unmounted racks?

Dimensions: 12" high; 8" wide

## CUTTING LIST

| Key | Part | Dimensions | Pcs. | Material |
|-----|------|------------|------|----------|
| A | Oval shape jar/vase | 2" x 6-8" x 12" | 1 | Glass |

**Materials:** Flat rocks of various sizes and shapes; antlers from a small deer rack; thinset bonding mortar mix, 3–5 lb. premix container or small 5 or 10-lb bag; green felt; glass adhesive; small piece of Styrofoam.

**Directions:**

1. Mix up a small batch of a gray thinset bonding mortar following the manufacturer's directions. Most simply require adding water. Premade mixes are also available in small containers. Both are available at your local tile supply store or a major supplier such as Home Depot or Lowe's.

2. Using the scraper or simply use your hands with a pair of rubber or latex gloves, start applying the mortar mix to the bottom portion of the jar or vase. Apply so it is approximately 3/16" thick.

3. Start applying the stones and rocks into the mortar mix following your design.

Continue applying the mortar mix and the antler until you complete coverage up to the top of the jar or vase.

4. Allow the mortar to dry overnight.

5. Turn the jar or vase over, so the bottom is upright. Apply a small amount of glass adhesive to the glass, and place the felt into the adhesive. Allow to dry. Using a utility knife, cut the excess felt from around the bottom.

6. Using a utility knife, cut pieces of Styrofoam so they fit into the bottom of the jar or vase. Since the top opening is smaller than the bottom, it will be possible to lay out several pieces on the bottom. Place a small amount of glass adhesive to the bottom of the jar or vase and place the Styrofoam pieces onto the adhesive along the bottom.

# 24

# ARCHER'S TOILET PAPER HOLDER

## TOOLS

Hand saw or table saw

Drill; 1/8" and 1/4" drill bit

Screw gun

Carpenter's square

Jigsaw

T his toilet paper holder gives your hunting camp the ambiance of a bowhunter's lodge. The frame is made of poplar and paint-ed a nice forest green. It makes use of old, unused arrows that I had lying around for years, as I am constantly changing my arrows and broadheads.

I cut the arrow to the desired length to match the width of this paper holder, and inserted new broadhead inserts. The broadhead used is actually the plastic practice broadheads made by NAP RazorBack. Do not use actual broadheads, for obvious reasons. The arrow used is one of my original graphite Beman arrows that no longer matched my new bow.

One word of advice, don't put this in your home lavatory. There aren't many women I know who would appreciate something quite so rustic!

Dimensions: 10 5/8" long : 4" wide

---

## CUTTING LIST

| Key | Part | Dimensions | Pcs. | Material |
|-----|------|-----------|------|----------|
| A | Holder back plate | 3/4" x 4" x 24 3/4" | 1 | Poplar |
| B | Holder side plates | 3/4" x 4" x 5" | 2 | Poplar |

---

**Materials:** One arrow approximately 16" long; plastic RazorBack broadhead (any broadhead with dulled blades or even a target tip can be used instead); four 1 1/2" wood screws; two 2 1/2" brass wood screws.

### Directions:

1. Measure and cut pieces (A) and (B) as shown in cutting list. Use a hand saw and miter box or table saw to get true cuts.

2. Round the edges of the holder back plate (A) and the side plate (B) as shown in Figure 1 and 2, using a jigsaw.

3. Measure 1 3/4" from each end of the holder back plate and mark a pencil line using a carpenter's square.

4. Using a drill with a 1/8" bit, drill two holes along each line. Place a tab of wood glue on the end of the holder side plate (B); secure the plate to the holder back plate using two 1 1/2" wood screws and a screw gun. Repeat for the other side plate.

5. Drill a 1/4" hole in each of the side plates, as shown in Figure 2.

6. Depending on the arrow shaft used, cut it to the desired length. In this design the arrow should be at least 16" long. Slip the front of the arrow through the hole and through the other end. Screw in the desired broadhead. Use any broadhead, but make sure that all sharp edges are removed to prevent anyone from cutting themselves. We used a plastic practice broadhead made by RazorBack broadheads.

7. Finish the holder with any paint, stain, or varnish of your choice. We used hunter green paint and applied two coats.

8. The holder's installed location will determine how it is mounted. If mounting on a standard framed drywall wall, drill two holes in the center, one close to the top and one at the bottom of the back plate. Align the holder holes along a stud and mount to the wall using two 2 1/2" brass wood screws.

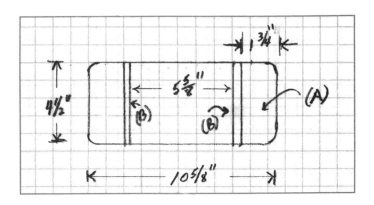

Figure 1 - Front View

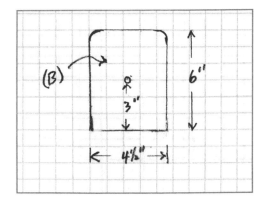

Figure 2 - Side View

# 25

# ARCHER'S TOWEL RACK

**TOOLS**

Hand saw or table saw

Drill; 1/8" and 1/4" drill bit

Screw gun

Carpenter's square

Jigsaw

This towel rack matches the archer's toilet paper holder from the previous chapter. The frame is made out of poplar and painted a nice forest green. It makes use of old, unused arrows that I had lying around for years, as I am constantly changing my arrows and broadheads.

I cut the arrow to the desired length to match the width of the towel rack and inserted new broadhead inserts. The broadhead used is actually the plastic practice broadheads made by RazorBack Five. Do not use actual broadheads for obvious reasons. The arrow used is one of my original graphite Beman arrows that no longer matched my new bow.

Dimensions: 24 3/4" long; 4" wide

## CUTTING LIST

| Key | Part | Dimensions | Pcs. | Material |
|-----|------|------------|------|----------|
| A | Towel back plate | 3/4" x 4" x 24 3/4" | 1 | Poplar |
| B | Towel side plate | 3/4" x 4" x 5" | 2 | Poplar |

**Materials:** One arrow approximately 28" long; plastic RazorBack broadhead (any broadhead with dulled blades or even a target tip can be used instead); four 1 1/2" wood screws, two 2 1/2" brass wood screws.

## Directions:

1. Measure and cut pieces (A), and (B) as shown in cutting list. Use a hand saw and miter box or table saw to get true cuts.

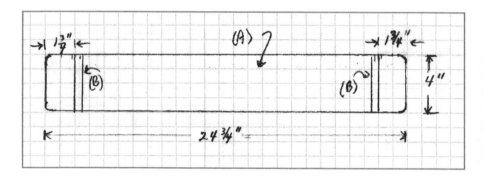

Figure 1 - Front View

2. Round the edges of the towel back plate (A) and the side plate (B), as shown in Figure 1 and 2, using a jigsaw.

3. Measure 1 3/4" from each end of the towel back plate and mark a pencil line using a carpenter's square.

4. Using a drill with a 1/8" bit, drill two holes along each line. Place a dab of wood glue on the end of the towel side plate (B); secure the plate to the towel back plate using two 1 1/2" wood screws and a screw gun. Repeat for the other side plate.

5. Drill a 1/4" hole in each of the side plates, as shown in Figure 2.

6. Cut the arrow shaft to the desired length. In this design, the arrow should be at least 28" long. Slip the front of the arrow through the hole and through the other end. Screw in the desired broadhead. Use any broadhead, but make sure that all sharp edges are removed to prevent people from cutting themselves. We used a plastic practice broadhead made by RazorBack Five.

7. Finish with any paint, stain, or varnish of your choice. We used hunter green paint and applied two coats.

8. Where the rack is installed will determine how it is mounted. If you're mounting it on a standard frame drywall wall, drill two holes at 16" centers. Mount to the wall using 2 1/2" brass wood screws.

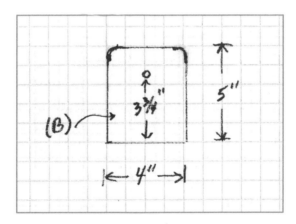

Figure 2 - Side View

# 26

# ARCHER'S LAMP

## TOOLS

Table saw

Drill with 1/8" and 1/4" bits

Screw gun

Carpenter's square

Router with Classic Roman ogee bit 1/8" radius x 1/2" high

Palm sander

1/2" wood chisel

Lamp

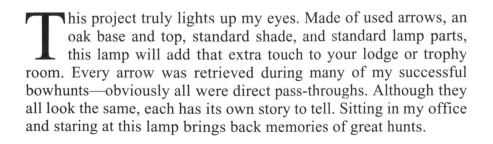

This project truly lights up my eyes. Made of used arrows, an oak base and top, standard shade, and standard lamp parts, this lamp will add that extra touch to your lodge or trophy room. Every arrow was retrieved during many of my successful bowhunts—obviously all were direct pass-throughs. Although they all look the same, each has its own story to tell. Sitting in my office and staring at this lamp brings back memories of great hunts.

The base and top plate were finished with clear satin polyurethane, showing the detail of the oak. Other woods can be used, and stained, varnished, or painted.

Save your used or old arrows for this project. The length of the arrows and the subsequent height of the lamp can be made shorter or longer to meet your design and décor. Standard lamp parts can be purchased in any local hardware store or a major store such as Home Depot. The shade used here is a simple off-white color. Other styles are available; just do a Google search for shades and you will be amazed at the selection and styles available at an endless list of stores. Don't be surprised to see them at stores such as Gander Mountain or Cabela's.

Try this project at home. It is simple, practical, and makes use of old arrows lying around. Some of my arrows were more than 15 years old. Standard target tips were used, but old dulled broadheads also work.

Dimensions: 40" high: 7 1/2" wide

## CUTTING LIST

| Key | Part | Dimensions | Pcs. | Material |
|-----|------|-----------|------|----------|
| A | Top Plate | 3/4" x 5 1/2" x 5 1/2" | 1 | Oak |
| B | Bottom plate | 3/4" x 5 1/2" x 5 1/2" | 1 | Oak |
| C | Lamp base | 3/4" x 7 1/2" x 7 1/2" | 1 | Oak |

**Materials:** One 30" threaded 3/8" lamp rod; one push thru bottom out socket; four 3/8" hex nuts brass; two 3/4" brass washers; one 8" harp; one 1/2" finial; one 8' opaque gold cord set; lamp shade. Eight 26 1/4" arrows with target tips.

**Directions:**

1. Measure and cut pieces (A), (B), and (C) as shown in the cutting list. Use a table saw to get true cuts.

2. Using a router with a Classic Roman ogee bit, finish off one edge of the top plate (A), bottom plate (B), and the lamp base (C). Sand smooth using a palm sander.

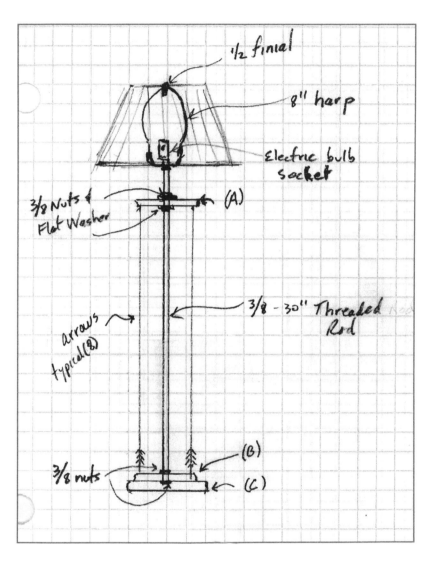

The following labels appear on the drawing:

- ½ finial
- 8" harp
- Electric bulb socket
- 3/8 Nuts & Flat Washer
- (A)
- 3/8 - 30" Threaded Rod
- arrows typical (8)
- (B)
- (C)
- 3/8 nuts

Figure 1 - Side View

177

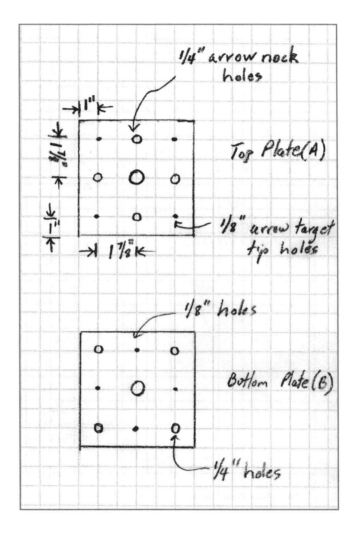

Figure 2 - Top and Bottom Views

178

3. Drill a 3/8" hole in the center of all three wood plates and base. Drill 1/8" holes, 1/2" deep in the top and bottom plates at the locations shown in Figure 2. Drill 1/4" holes, 1/2" deep in the remaining eight locations.

4. Using a wood chisel, notch out a 1/2" square around the center hole of the bottom base approximately 1/4" deep.

5. Attach the threaded rod to the bottom plate (B) using one 3/8" nut on the bottom and another one on the top side of the plate. Tighten securely using a pair of pliers or socket wrench. Refer to Figure 1 for details.

6. Secure the bottom plate to the lamp base (C), centering it so the threaded rod aligns with the center hole of the lamp base. Use wood glue and screws from the bottom with four 1 1/4" wood screws.

7. Apply a finish of your choice to the top, the bottom plates, and the lamp base. We used a clear finish.

8. Place a 3/8" nut, then a flat washer approximately 3" from the top of the threaded rod.

9. Position the arrows, as shown in Figure 2, into the holes of the bottom plate. Slip the top plate (A) over the top of the threaded rod. Position the arrows into the holes of the top plate.

10. Place another flat washer over the rod and another 3/8" nut, and tighten until the washer is flush and the top plate is tightly secured in place.

11. Place another 3/8" washer on the top of the threaded rod 1/2" down. Place the 8" harp over the rod so it lies on top of the nut. Screw on the socket to the top of the rod. Tighten until it secures the harp in place. Tighten up the set screw.

12. Slip the end of the cord setup from the bottom through the threaded rod so it comes out the top. Attach the wire to the terminals of the socket. Slip the socket in place.

13. Attach the shade of your choice and secure it using a 1/2" finial.

Here's a fun twist on the pegboard game often found in roadside rest stops to help folks pass the time while they wait for their food.

# 27

# PEGBOARD GAME

There are many puzzle games, but this simple pegboard game is one of my favorites. Some know it as Strategy; we just call it the arrow shaft pegboard game.

No matter what it's called, this is a challenging pegboard game for one player. Start with any one hole open and proceed by jumping over pegs as in checkers, removing those pegs that are jumped. The objective is to finish with just one peg left. Since there are 15 different holes that can be the starting open hole, there are many different solutions. One variation to make the challenge more difficult is to try to end up with the last peg in the starting open hole. This is for kids ages 5 to adults.

This simple project makes a perfect desktop addition. It is very easy to make. Again, we made use of some old arrows. The shafts were cut to the desired lengths, new inserts and target tips were installed, and there you have the game. Keep it on your desk and when things get slow at work or you need a break, play a few games.

Dimensions: 8 1/4" x 8 1/4" x 8 1/4"

---

### CUTTING LIST

| Key | Part | Dimensions | Pcs. | Material |
|-----|------|-----------|------|----------|
| A | Board | 8 1/4" x 8 1/4" x 8 1/4" | 1 | Oak |

---

**Materials:** 15 cut ends of arrows with inserts and target tips; sandpaper.

Note: Measurements reflect the actual thickness of dimension lumber.

**Directions:**

1. Cut the triangular shape of the pegboard using a table saw or hand saw. Round off the edges using sandpaper or a palm sander.

2. Refer to Figure 1, and lay out the hole pattern on the board. Using an awl and hammer, make a hole at each location to assist in guiding the drill bit.

3. Using a drill and 1/4" drill bit, make holes at each location 1/2" deep. Use a drill stop or simply tape the end of the drill bit to act as a stop 1/2" up the bit.

4. Cut the shaft ends of old arrows so that approximately 1-2 inches extends past the fletching. The arrows can be cut using an arrow cutter or a hacksaw. Glue arrow inserts in each of the arrow tips and screw in the practice tips.

5. You are now ready to play.

# 28

# VARIOUS ANTLER PROJECTS

T he following projects were made from antlers of deer and elk harvested over a period of years during many bowhunts. Some antlers were found while shed hunting during the off-season. Tools needed include a hand drill with various drill bits; a power miter box with a carbide tooth blade or hacksaw; a hand miter box or bandsaw to cut the antler pieces; a grinding wheel; a workbench with a vise; a small metal file; a wooden rasp; and a palm sander or belt sander to smooth the surfaces and edges. Tools used for making the wooden plaque for the hat rack included a jigsaw and router to shape the edges. Materials needed obviously required antlers, and two-part epoxy mix, stain, varnish, shellac, or clear water-based satin finish, and wood screws.

## LETTER OPENER/EATING UTENSILS

I added a section of deer antler to an existing letter opener to make a nice-looking handle. I used a piece of a shed antler I found during the off-season. You can also opt to make a blade from a piece of steel by grinding it down into the shape of the opener shown here. A metal grinding wheel will be needed. Using a bandsaw, hacksaw, and/or a miter box, cut the end of an antler approximately 5 or 6". To make the

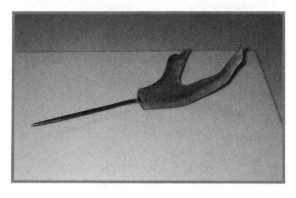

cutout in the base of the antler, use a small drill with a 1/8" bit. Place the antler in a small vise, wrapping it with a piece of cardboard or rag to prevent scratching the antler. Drill a series of small holes at least 1" deep along the center of the antler base, slightly longer than the end of the letter opener or cut piece of steel. Use a small flat file to smooth the opening and then try fitting the end into the opening. Make up a mixture of two-part epoxy and pour it into the open end of the antler. Slip the end of the letter opener into the hole and position it so it lies squarely into the hole and lines up horizontally with the handle. Wipe off the excess epoxy with a rag and allow to dry. The handle can be left as is, or buffed with sandpaper or steel wool and then finished with a shellac or varnish for a glossy smooth finish. Following the same procedure as described above, you can easily make eating utensils such as a knife, fork, or spoon using a set of your wife's less favorite kitchen utensils.

## DOORKNOBS AND DOOR HANDLE

The following projects were made from an elk antler. Knobs are easy to make by simply cutting small sections beginning from the end or base of the antler. Using a radial arm saw, bandsaw, hacksaw and/or a miter box, cut the end of an antler. Cut at lengths approximately 3/4" or longer as desired. Smooth the ends using a belt sander or palm sander. Place one end into a vise so that the cut end faces up and drill a 1/16" pilot hole about 1/2" to 3/4" deep depending on the overall length of the knob. Drill an 1/8" hole in the center of the drawer or cabinet door, use a panhead screw (about 1 1/2" for a 3/4" drawer or door face), and mount the knob by inserting the screw from the inside face. Screw tightly into the knob. The knob can be left as is or finished with a stain, shellac or varnish for a glossy smooth finish.

Handles can also be made. Here we used small cut sections from a deer antler. Using a radial arm saw, band-saw, or hacksaw and a miter box cut a section of an antler approximately 5 to 6" long.

Flatten the ends using a belt sander, then round off the ends to avoid sharp edges. Cut two more pieces approximately 1 to 1 1/2" long, which are used to extend the handle from the cabinet door or drawer face. Make sure that one end of each piece is cut square. Use a belt sander or wooden rasp to round off the other end slightly to match the contour of the longer handle piece where they meet (see photo). Set the long piece on top of both short pieces on your workbench. Align the curved end of the short piece in the desired location against the long handle. Use a wooden clamp to hold the assembly in place. Use a drill with a 3/16" to 1/4" bit to make a hole through the front face and the short piece. Repeat for the other side. Use a brass or chrome pan-head wood screw long enough to fit through the face of the long piece, the short piece, and into the wooden door face allowing approximately 1/2" to mount the handle to the door or drawer surface. The handle can be left as is, or buffed with sandpaper or steel wool, and then finished with a stain, shellac, or varnish for a glossy smooth finish.

## BUCKLES, BUTTONS, TIE PINS, AND KEY RING

Sections of whitetail antlers cut into thin slices produced the following projects. A belt buckle was made by cutting the base end of an antler. Use a section that measures at least 1 1/2" in diameter. Using a radial arm saw, bandsaw, or hacksaw and miter box, cut a slice approximately 1/4" to 3/8" thick. Using a two-part epoxy mixture, glue this piece to the face of a plain metal buckle attached to an existing belt.

Follow this same procedure to make buttons. Cut slices approximately 1/8" thick and 3/8" in diameter. Place them into a vise and drill four small holes in the center of each button. Maybe someone special can take over here and sew them onto your favorite shirt.

Again, follow the same procedure as above and cut a slice approximately 1/4" thick and 1/4" to 3/8" in diameter. Obtain the back pin from an old unused tie pin. Drill a tiny hole (slightly smaller than the diameter of the pin) into the backside of the slice halfway through. Check to make sure that the tie pin fits snugly into the back of the antler tie pin. If not, cut another slice and make sure the hole is made smaller.

Cut a 3- to 4-inch section of antler from the base to make this handy key ring. Drill a 1/4-inch hole at the base end. Use a 3-inch key ring (or other size as desired) and slip the open end into the hole. Insert your keys and close the key ring.

All the above can be left as is, or buffed with sand paper or steel wool, and then finished with a shellac or varnish for a glossy smooth finish.

## MATCHSTICK AND TOOTHPICK HOLDER

Using sections from wider antlers such as from an elk rack or larger, handy projects such as these can be made. Cut sections approximately 4-6" long from the thickest part of the elk antler. Place the cut section into a vise and drill a hole using a 1/2" bit approximately 3-4" deep. The holder can be left as is, or buffed with sandpaper or steel wool, and then finished with a shellac or varnish for a glossy smooth finish. Place the matchsticks in the

holder and display next to your fireplace. Follow the same procedure as above using a shorter section of antler to make a toothpick holder.

# TIE RACK

For this handy project, a section of a deer antler was used. Cut this section approximately 10 to 12" long using a radial arm saw, hacksaw, or bandsaw. Smooth the ends using a belt sander or palm sander. Mark four locations approximately 1 1/4" apart in the center along the antler on the front side.

Using a drill and 1/8" bit, make holes at those locations approximately 1/2" deep. Screw four Shaker pegs with screw #10- 7/8" x 3" long into the holes. Stain and finish the wooden pegs as desired. Drill two 3/16" mounting holes at each end to mount the tic rack in your closet. Using brass screws long enough to fit through the antler, the wall, plus at least 1" longer to penetrate the wooden stud, mount the rack to the wall and hang your favorite ties. This particular antler had a natural finish, therefore no shellac or varnish was necessary.

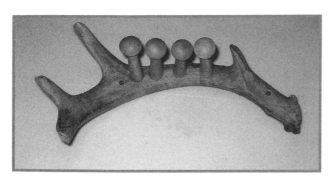

## BOW RACK

This project made use of a section of an elk antler approximately 24" long with enough points to hang four or five hats. A piece of wood 10" wide by 36" long was used to shape into a curved arrow. The antler section was placed on the board and the curved portion of the antler was traced. Using a jigsaw, cut out

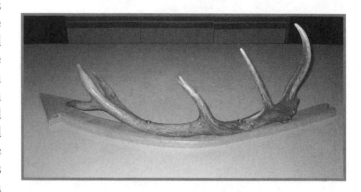

the shape as shown in the finished project. Finish the edges using a router with a 1/4" round bit for the shaft section and nock. Using a 1/4" beveled router bit, cut the edge on the broadhead end. Sand smooth using a palm sander or sand by hand. Finish the wooden arrow as desired. Place the antler section on the board so that the points will face perpendicularly. Drill two 3/16" holes through the antler about 16" apart. Use wood screws to mount the antler to the arrow board. In case you are wondering, I shaped the arrow as shown to remind me of the arrow used to take this elk. My shot was quartering away, and the arrow went through the lungs, but hit the shoulder on the other side and bent just as shown here. Mount it on the wall and use it to hang your bows after a day afield.

## ANTLER DISPLAYS

Several years of successful bowhunts and accumulating various racks allowed me to make this nice antler display. It starts with a few ten-point racks and descends to a small six-pointer. Place the larger rack as the base, add each smaller rack into the larger rack, and tie together with 20-gauge wire until all pieces are secured in place.

# 29

# PLANTING TIPS TO ATTRACT & HOLD WILDLIFE

This chapter is meant to provide DIY ideas to help you plant and grow food plots to attract and hold deer on your land from November to January—the time of year most hunters want to have deer feeding in their food plots! The plants I strongly recommend to achieve this goal are mostly in the brassica family, plus a few other plantings. The brassicas include purple-top turnips, forage rape and kale, and canola. The other winter-hardy plants include Kura clover—and my favorite: sugar beets.

For those who have never planted a food plot before, I have included some basic planting points. With that said, however, the following information is less about "how to" and much more about which winter-hardy plants will draw deer to your land in November, December and January.

The plants I've mentioned are easy to grow, and require the least amount of work to maintain. One of the most attractive points about each of them is that they can be grown in plots as small as a fifth of an acre or in much larger plots, from one acre in size and up.

In planting your food plots, remember the adage, "The right tools make the job easier." When it comes to playing in the dirt, this phrase is worth repeating to yourself before you plant a single seed! If you believe that you can successfully plant healthy crops that will produce quality nutrition for deer by simply broadcasting seeds over hard ground—forget what you may have heard! All seeds do best on ground that has been properly prepared, so that they can grow to their maximum potential.

## KNOW YOUR PH LEVEL

For optimum results with the plants that are recommended here, the pH level of your soil should be between 5.9 and 6.5—that is, slightly acidic; 7 being neutral on the pH scale and levels higher than 7 being increasingly alkaline. Therefore, it is important that you test your soil to make sure its pH is at the correct level prior to planting.

An ATV-mounted sprayer unit works well to apply herbicide on food plots 5 acres and less.

In calculating pH levels, which involves measuring humic matter and exchangeable acidity levels, a soil test will determine if lime is needed and, if so, how much to apply to the soil. Don't guess how much lime to add. These plants don't do as well when the pH is level is too high (above 6.6). In fact, a high pH may block plants' ability to absorb vital nutrients, such as iron, manganese, boron, copper and zinc, which in turn will affect deer nutrition, size, and quality.

Start by taking a small soil sample of each area you intend to plant. Then, send the samples to your local farm supply dealer, county extension service or even a seed company that provides pH testing. You do not need a lot of soil; most places only test a tablespoon to get the pH level. By simply using a soil sample report, you will be able to eliminate the guesswork. Some food-plot planters whose soil is very acidic don't realize just how much lime it takes to raise the pH levels: a few tons per acre! So even in small plots, you may have to apply several 100-lb. bags of lime to the soil to get it ready for planting.

## USING HERBICIDES

No matter what type of seeds you plant, they will grow much better if you control the weeds in the plot. Before planting, spray the plot to kill both grasses and broadleaf weeds. Herbicides work best when the weather is warm and dry for at least a few days after spraying, and you will have to wait at least a week before planting after you spray any herbicide.

## USING FERTILIZER

Each of the crops in this chapter will grow better when fertilized with a blend of nitrogen, phosphorus and potassium—also known as N-P- K. The correct fertilizer mix will help the crops grow to their maximum potential. For instance, an average one-acre plot of turnips requires about 200 pounds or more of 19-19-19 (meaning that for every 100 pounds of fertilizer there are 19 pounds of nitrogen, 19 pounds of phosphorus and 19 pounds of potassium) topped off with about 100 pounds of ammonium sulfate. Nitrogen is the key element for plant protein production. Potassium and phosphorus are essential building-block elements for antler growth, bone, milk and body growth for deer. Including these elements in your soil is important not only for the plants, but the deer as well.

## PLANTING BY HAND & ATV

If you plant only several really small areas (one-tenth of an acre or 4,330 square feet), the plots can be effectively worked using a combination of hand tools and an ATV The equipment needed for hand planting includes:

• A quality three-gallon herbicide hand-held sprayer or a backpack sprayer

• A sturdy, heavy-duty push spreader with at least a 75-lb. capacity to spread the seeds and fertilizer on the plots

• A stout iron rake with steel teeth to smooth out the plot

A push-type or hand-held seeder can also be used to spread seed or fertilizer in smaller-food plots.

That is the practical limit for the hand-held equipment. In addition, you will need a small ATV (400 ccs or so) that will comfortably pull a small disc (tiller) and a chain drag harrow to smooth out the plot.

## DEER-BARRIER SYSTEMS

Small plots can be quickly and easily over-browsed by deer. To lessen the potential damage, you should either plant a "nurse crop" (like a winter-hardy clover) near them to prevent deer from over-browsing the plot, or use a deer-barrier system.

I have used the Plot Saver Deer Barrier System and find it works well to deter deer from getting into my small plots, at least temporarily, so my plants can reach maturity. It is a lot less expensive than using a high-fence system. All you have to do is place the stakes that come with the kit around the area you want to protect, stretch the three-quarter-inch Plot Saver Ribbon around the perimeter and spray the ribbon with Plot Saver deer-repellent formula. Each application is effective for about two to three days—sometimes longer—and the system comes with enough repellent to keep deer away for 100 days.

This photo shows a foodplot that was staked out with a Plot Saver Ribbon (on the left) and the same plants were planted without the ribbon on the right. (photo courtesy PlotSaver)

An 840-foot spool of the braided Plot Saver Ribbon, an absorbent poly-tape that lasts approximately six years, is included in the kit (enough for one acre) as well as a 16-ounce bottle of Plot Saver Concentrate. The system can be purchased in most sporting-goods stores, all the big catalog stores and online at www.plotsaver.com. Fiberglass stakes (not included), which are 39" tall and come with clips to hold the ribbon in place at the optimum height of 30", and an extra 16-ounce bottle of concentrate also are available at the same locations.

# ATVS

If you plan to plant in plots that are at least one-tenth of an acre and up, the reality is that you will need to make an investment to purchase more heavy-duty equipment: an ATV with at least 500 ccs or more of power, if you can afford it. A hefty ATV can pull a one- or two-row plow, a heavier disc, a larger chain-drag harrow, a small brush hog, grass cutter, seeder, herbicide sprayer, compactor and other implements without over straining the engine.

Here I transport heavy seed bags and some started plants in the back of my ArcticCat ATV to one of our food plots. I use the tractor and compactor/seeder to plant seeds in larger plots while my son Cody plants the started pumpkins in a nearbyplot.

I highly recommend Arctic Cat ATVs and their entire line of food-plot implements for both large and small plots. The company designed their planting implement equipment specifically to be used with their line of ATVs, and after using them successfully for years when planting my property, Arctic Cat quads and planting equipment remain my first choice. Don't kid yourself. If you're going to plant wildlife food plots seriously and don't have either the budget or the need for a tractor, your only logical choice is an ATV with an array of implements to get the job done right.

Because accomplishing work on the farm totally depends on equipment that is reliable, durable and affordable, you may also want to include a good utility ATV that will hold plenty of planting equipment (shovels, rakes, bags of seed, fertilizer, lime, etc.). Later in the year, that utility vehicle comes in handy to carry hunting equipment, hunters, and harvested deer, too. You will get years of service from utility ATVs—our Prowler fits in all those categories and is a "workhorse" of a machine. As an added bonus, they are also capable of pulling most planting attachments.

Pay your favorite ATV dealer a visit. He will give you the best advice available and help you make the right choice in purchasing the type of equipment that will work best for your land, needs and budget.

Now that you have chosen the type of equipment for creating a food plot, there are very specific steps you must take before planting even a single seed.

## WHAT TO PLANT

Now it is time to get down to the crux of this chapter. As I said at the start, the plants I suggest (purple-top turnips, grain sorghum, forage rape and kale, forage chicory, Kura clover and sugar beets) will all do well in small or large-sized plots.

Grain sorghum is a terrific plant to replace corn. It is much less expensive and offers equal cover and nutrition when compared to corn for deer and it is much easier to plant and grow.

Think about this for a moment: Your neighbors and nearby hunting clubs are not likely to be growing most of the plants I've mentioned. If they have food plots, they are probably planting mostly clovers, although some may also include chicory and turnips, and local farmers are most likely growing plenty of corn, clovers, timothy, soybeans, etc. By planting the different types of crops I've named, you will entice deer to your property from surrounding lands, and keep your resident herd from leaving your property.

It is important to mention here that if you have several fields available to plant and you have the equipment, time and money to plant them all, then you may also want to include other winter-hardy plants, such as corn, Austrian winter peas, birdsfoot trefoil, and the small grains like winter wheat and winter rye (which should not be confused with perennial ryegrass). Remember, these plants require large plots of an acre or two in size to grow to their full potential.

I stopped planting corn for a variety of reasons. First, every farmer around me has a majority of his land planted in corn, so the deer have enough of it to eat. Second, corn is very expensive. A bag of Round-Up Ready Corn in 2010 costs more than $225! On top of that, it requires an expensive piece of machinery to plant it correctly—a one- or two-row planter for small acreage and a larger one if you plant more than 10 acres of corn. Then, you have to buy a lot of lime and nitrogen to keep it growing well. And you have to buy herbicide to keep the weeds from overtaking the crop.

In other words, planting corn is expensive, time-consuming and a lot of hard work. Grain sorghum, on the other hand, is much less expensive, requires much less maintenance, and I have found it is more attractive to deer—especially if corn is grown all around you!

## FORAGE RAPE

Forage Rape is a cold-weather brassica and, like other brassicas—such as kale, turnips, cabbage, canola, radish, Swede and rutabaga—its leafy greens work well to draw deer to food plots throughout most of the United States and Canada.

During my 30 years of planting food plots, I have found that forage rape and kale are among the easiest to plant and maintain. Deer will browse the rape leaves in summer, but they really don't hit the plant hard until there are a few hard frosts in late fall, which is why

Here is a plot of forage rape planted at the base of a hill with one of our tree stands nearby.

I would not go a season without planting several small (one-quarter acre to one full acre) plots of forage rape on my farm.

To give rape the best start possible, it must be planted early. In the North, I suggest planting it anytime after the 4th of July. Rape is ready to browse from 30 to 90 days after it has established itself. In the South, it should be planted no later than September for best results.

For optimal production, plant rape in a plot that has good soil drainage. While rape will tolerate pH levels between 5.5 and 6.5, it does best in soil with a pH of 6.0. Rape seed is tiny, and like all tiny seed plants, it can be successfully top-sown on bare soil. However, I prefer top-sowing on soil that has been tilled. In either case, plant your rape crop just prior to a forecasted rainfall for best germination.

First, till your soil no deeper than three inches to help keep the weeds down. Tilling the soil deeper only stimulates weed growth. Use a combination of herbicides to kill unwanted grass, broadleaf and other noxious weeds. Be careful to follow all instructions exactly and wait to plant according to the directions as well. I like to use herbicides after the weeds begin to emerge and are three inches high or so. Whatever the date is that I plan to plant, I spray my herbicides at least a full week beforehand.

197

Plant five to 10 pounds lbs. of forage rape seed per acre. If your plot is smaller than an acre, calculate its square footage by measuring and multiplying the length of its sides, then divide that total by 43,560 (which is the total square footage of an acre) to get the size of your plot in acres. That will help you break down approximately how much fertilizer and/or seed is required for each plot you plant. Be sure not to over-seed. Planting more seed than recommended accounts for more plot failures than planting less! This fact is true of all plantings.

I like to plant most of my food plots with just one seed. Sometimes I mix them, but when it comes to brassicas, I prefer to plant them alone or near a nurse crop of the winter-hardy clover— Kura. I plant this legume close by to take the browsing pressure off my other plants during the summer months.

Make sure that you achieve good soil-to-seed contact. Using a compactor will help. Short of that, you can ride an ATV over the seeded plot very slowly to help press the seed into the ground.

To get the best production and forage, fertilize as you're planting with 300 lbs. of 19-19-19 per acre and 100 lbs. per acre of 34-0-0. When properly fertilized, rape leaves will have crude protein levels that are between 15 to 30 percent. The total digestibility nutrients (TDN) could reach 60 to 75 percent, with a dry matter reaching about 10 to 15 percent. Basically, rape rates highly as a very digestible forage for deer.

Like the other brassicas I mentioned, you will discover that deer will seek out forage rape very enthusiastically from November through January! You will be surprised how many deer will visit the plot even during daylight hours in the hunting season—and that is true for all brassica plots.

## FORAGE KALE

Kale is among the top three fall forage brassicas, with crude protein levels ranging from about 15 to 28 percent. The only downside to kale is that it is a slower growing plant than turnips and rape. If you plant kale, you have to allow at least four months for it to grow to maturity, or about 100 to 150 days.

Forage kale grows well in cool areas and, in fact, will produce best in northern zones. It should be planted in June or July—about four to five lbs. per acre. If you plant smaller plots, calculate their size in acres (using the method explained in the forage rape section) to help you estimate how much fertilizer and/or seed is required for each plot you plant. Kale should not be planted deeper than one-quarter inch under the soil. With that said, however, let me add that I have had excellent success top-seeding the tiny seeds of kale.

Kale grows well when the pH level is between 5.9 and 6.6. If the pH gets too high the leaves will begin to molt. Like the other brassicas, forage kale should be fertilized with at least 300 lbs. of T 19-19-19 when you plant it. You should also include two to four pounds of boron, 50 to 100 pounds of magnesium, and one-eighth to one-fifth of a pound of copper and zinc—especially if your soil test suggests they are necessary.

I use a variety called Maris Kestrel kale, but there are many types of forage kale available. Because kale is a slow grower, I often split the plot in half with rape on one side and kale on the other. Again, in very small plots, it is advisable to include a nurse crop of Kura clover to prevent deer from over-browsing the brassica plantings.

Kale is easy to plant and maintain. It will provide forage when you most want it...during the hunting season. As soon as there have been a couple of deep freezes, deer will march into your kale stand with a serious intent to eat as much as they can. I plant about an acre or more each year and I'm never disappointed by how it attracts deer to my land or by the results during the hunting season. Once you plant kale and witness the use by deer in winter, it will become a vital part of your yearly plantings, too.

## SUGAR BEETS

There is a good reason why I say (without hesitation) that my favorite food-plot planting is sugar beets. Nothing else I have ever planted over the last 30 years has worked better to draw deer into my plots and hold them there during the hunting season.

Deer simply go "bonkers" for sugar beets once they discover what they are. Even when the plot is covered with snow, deer still actively seek them out, pawing up the snow until they unearth the tasty treat. As far as deer are concerned, sugar beets are ice-cream! Many times I have seen the same group of does or individual bucks returning to a sugar beet plot several times in one day!

Once there have been several hard frosts by mid-November, deer will enthusiastically and relentlessly dig for sugar beets in a plot until they have devoured each and every one of them.

During the 2009 deer season on our farm in New York, the regular firearm season proved to be frustrating. The weather was milder than normal and we had a hard time seeing good bucks the entire three weeks of the rifle season. It wasn't until two days before the muzzleloader season opened that the temperatures dipped dramatically. For the next couple of days after opening day of muzzleloader season, it snowed and the thermometer didn't climb much over single digits.

My son P. Cody with a sugar beet from one of our food plots. It had been dug up by a deer in late December.

That was all it took for the sugar beets to "sweeten-up" and become a primary food source for the deer on our place. The sugar beet field looked like the deer were digging them up with shovels. By the third day of the season, I shot a dandy 8-point buck with a 21-inch plus inside spread at 11 am. He came into the sugar beet plot with a group of does.

Only two-and-a-half days later, Jeff Elliott, the CEO of Coventry Log Homes, shot another terrific buck in the same sugar beet plot at 1:30 p.m. Jeff said he had watched well over a dozen deer come in and out of the plot all morning. When he saw his 9-point buck come in, he didn't waste a second before putting the crosshairs on him (see photo on p. 202)!

In less than a week, two good bucks were taken after not seeing a "keeper" buck for three weeks prior to that. Clearly, if you want to see deer in your food plots from November to January, sugar beets must be a vital part of your late season list of plantings!

Some food plotters think that sugar beets are classified as a brassica. In fact, they are a biennial vegetable. What makes them a top-rated seed to plant, however, is that like any of the brassicas, sugar

This wide-antlered 8-point buck was taken as it dug through the snow to get a sugar beet in the plot just behind the corn during the late muzzleloader season in December.

beets are a cold-weather crop that makes a terrific, if not the best, attractant food plot for deer, especially during the critical periods of winter when deer are stressed to find quality foods.

Sugar beets have a very high digestibility rate. Some experts say they have the highest digestibility of any forage (95 percent), and I certainly wouldn't argue that point. Sugar beets have a protein content of 12 to 15 percent as well. While that isn't as high as many of the other plantings have, it is still noteworthy.

Because they have a short growing season of only 90 to 100 days, sugar beets can be planted in early spring or, for northern areas, in late June or early July. I plant my beets no later than the 4th of July. By the end of September, and no later than the first week of October, they have matured.

As the weather cools in the fall, the sugar content in the plant begins to increase. Usually, by mid-November, most northern climates have undergone a few hard freezes, which help to increase the sugar content of the roots even further and makes the plants more palatable to deer.

Jeff Elliott, President of Coventry Log Homes, shot this big 9-point buck as it was heading to a turnip plot in December!

The first time I planted sugar beets, I was surprised to discover that deer eat the tops of the plant as well. Speaking of that, don't mow the leaves of the sugar beets as they are growing. It will encourage additional leaf growth, which ends up decreasing the sugar content in the plant's root system—the key to attracting deer.

I have heard some folks tell me that it took "a couple of years" before their deer discovered sugar beets. If that is the case when you plant them, you may have to dig up a few to help the deer find out they like them (check your local game laws before doing this). Since the sugar beet itself sometimes sticks as much as halfway out of the ground, deer don't take long to learn that they love eating this plant.

Plant your beets in a medium-to-heavy, loamy soil that receives ample moisture. Be careful about the site you select, however. While the beets will need adequate water in the summer, as young plants they are vulnerable to drowning if they get too much water.

It is absolutely crucial to make sure that the plot you intend to plant sugar beets in is weed-free prior to planting the seeds in order to assure a successful crop. Once the plants begin to shoot up, their leaves will sufficiently block out the sun to prevent weed growth and competition. I spray my sugar beet plots thoroughly about two weeks before I intend to plant them with Pronto Big N' Tuf (available at Tractor Supply).

Before planting sugar beets, take a soil test to determine the exact pII level. If it is lower than 6.0 you will have to lime it heavily in order to get the pH level to 6.5 to 7.5, which sugar beets prefer.

You should also prepare the plot by fertilizing it with at least 400 lbs. of T-19 (19-19-19) per acre. Also plan to add about 20 lbs., per acre or so, of manganese sulfate. Till both fertilizers about three inches under the soil. When the plants are almost fully grown (about eight weeks later), broadcast with a push spreader about 100 lbs. of urea (46-0-0) per acre.

If your plot is smaller than an acre, calculate your seed, fertilizer and lime amounts by first measuring the plot accurately to break down approximately how much of each is required for that particular plot. (See the forage rape section.)

I try to plant my beets when there will be an expected rainfall. It is recommended that the seed is planted about one-quarter to one-half inches deep. They should be cultipacked well so they have good soil- to-seed contact. I have had very good success with top-sowing them and then using a compactor to press the seeds into the soil tightly. Either way has worked for me, but if you are planting sugar beets for the first time, you may want to stick with the seed-depth directions on the package.

There was a time when Roundup Ready sugar beets were available, but not as recently as this writing. The word is, however, that

Roundup Ready seeds will be in the works again soon. Before you purchase your seed, check to see if RR seeds are available. If they are, it will make your job of controlling weeds easier, even though it will cost more for the seed.

Remember that sugar beets have to be rotated each year. You can plant a winter-hardy clover like Kura or a winter wheat or rye in the plot the following year. Once you plant sugar beets and see how enthusiastically the deer feed on them, sugar beets will become a yearly crop that you will not want to do without.

# TURNIPS

Deer love to eat turnips, which are closely related to rutabagas and Swedes. What makes turnips desirable in a food plot is that they are classified as a cold-weather planting. The leaves of the turnip are also prized by deer from mid-September until January, adding to their value for early-fall bowhunters. The leaf tops have between 15 to 25 percent crude protein content. Even the plants' roots contain 10 to 15 percent protein. An acre of turnips can provide a crop anywhere from one to five tons per acre of dry matter, which includes the turnip bulb as well.

It may take one season for deer to "discover" what turnips are. But once they do, deer will become addicted and will seek them out feverishly as temperatures head south.

Turnips are an excellent choice as a food-plot planting for the colder regions of the Northeast, mid-West and other cold-weather areas of the country. They are also drought tolerant, which means they can be planted throughout the country and in Canada. Additionally, turnips can be planted late—in northern latitudes, they can be planted in July or early August; in southern regions, they can be planted in August or September—making them a terrific fall and winter crop. I find that planting them no later than the July 4th weekend gives them a longer growing period and helps them to fully mature 90 days before bow season in October.

Turnips like a slightly acidic soil pH between 5.9 and 6.5. I have had the most success when I plant them in medium loamy soil or heavy loamy soil. They will not do well, however, in wet ground or heavy clay soils.

Once deer find a field planted with turnips, it won't be long until you find half-eaten turnips like this everywhere!

Forage turnip seeds are tiny. There are a lot of different forage varieties to choose from. I like Purple Top and Royal Crown because they produce the largest turnip bulbs of all the varieties. Turnips are best seeded by using a quality drop seeder with strong wheels, a Pro Broadcast Spreader with a rain cover (it helps to keep the seed from bouncing out over rough ground), or a quality hand-operated Harvest Broadcast Spreader—all of which can be found at Tractor Supply stores.

Because of the tiny size of the seed, the plot should be tilled until the soil becomes a fine, firm seedbed. After tilling the plot, use a half-gallon glyphosate (per acre) to kill any emerging weeds. Wait at least five to seven days and then plant three to four pounds of turnip seed per acre. Turnips can be top-sown very successfully—especially just prior to an expected rainfall. If they are top-sown, make sure they make good soil-to-seed contact. If they are planted by drilling, don't cover them with soil any deeper than one-quarter inch.

As soon as they are planted, I like to fertilize them. For best results, use 400 lbs. of T-19 (Triple 19-19-19) per acre (300 pounds will work, too, if your budget is tight). About six weeks later, the plot should be top-dressed with about 100 to 200 pounds of ammonium sulfate (34-0-0) per acre. This will help increase the production of the plant and bulb. (Again, use the process explained in the forage rape section to determine how much is needed for any plot less than an acre.)

As I mentioned earlier, always get a soil test prior to planting any plot. If lime is needed to raise the pH, do so as early as possible before planting. Lime takes time to do its work. I also test to see which minerals are lacking in my soil. For instance, I discovered that my turnip plot was in need of boron and sulfur, and I had to add trace amounts of them to help my turnips. That is why I always recommend not skipping a soil test before planting.

When the plant gets to be about 10 inches high, deer will start eating it. It will take 90 to 120 days for turnips to fully mature. Unfortunately, if the deer graze on the turnip plants before then, they can hurt the production of both the tops and bulbs. That is why I like to plant an extremely winter-hardy clover (like Kura) near all my winter-hardy plants (sugar beets, turnips, kale, rape, canola, etc.). The succulent clover helps to distract and deflect the deer from eating my precious brassicas. I want them to be in prime condition from November to January, when I'm hunting deer!

You will find that turnips make a terrific crop and they will be an integral part of your winter-hardy planting program. Once the deer discover what they are, they won't leave them alone! But remember that all brassicas should not be planted in the same plot more than two consecutive years. It would be even better to rotate them yearly.

# CANOLA

Canola is a leafy brassica, and deer will eat it through the summer and from November to January. I have included canola in my food plots every year since I first planted it. I wouldn't go a season without it!

Canola requires at least a one-acre plot; it can not be planted in small plots or the deer will eat it long before it has a chance to get started. It is a fast-growing brassica that is actually a quality form of rape seed, and it has a high yield when planted as directed. Canola's leaves have a crude protein level that ranges from 20 to 30 percent—hard to beat when it comes to protein levels. The TDN (total digestible nutrients) can range from 50 to 75 percent dry matter, and the dry matter can be from 10 to 18 percent. Interestingly, when canola seeds are crushed, they contain up to 40 percent vegetable oil.

It is a cold-hardy fall plant that deer find especially attractive from October through January. I have found that deer will feed on both the stems and leaves as soon as the crop is ready to graze, which is about 60 to 90 days after planting.

In the North, canola can be planted in August or in early spring (April or May). In the South, it should be planted in September. Like most brassicas, it should not be planted in the same plot more than two consecutive years to prevent disease problems.

As with all brassicas, canola is cold tolerant, and this particular plant is also tolerant of drought and heat. It needs a plot that has good drainage, with a pH level between 5.5 and 7.5. It will do best, however, in soil with a pH of 6.0 to 7.5.

Prepare your canola plot by using a combination of herbicides to kill any emerged broadleaf weeds and grasses prior to planting. Wait two weeks and then till the soil as fine as possible. To prevent stimulating new weed growth, don't till the soil any deeper than three or four inches.

Like most brassicas, the canola seeds are tiny, and you'll have excellent success top-sowing them. Plant canola in a firm, well-tilled seed bed, then broadcast about eight pounds of seed to the acre. I find using a quality hand-pushed drop seeder with strong wheels, or a Pro

A field of canola that we planted in early May.

broadcast spreader with a rain cover (it helps to keep the seed from bouncing out over rough ground), or even a quality hand-operated Harvest Broadcast Spreader works best to plant tiny seeds. The seed must have good soil-to-seed contact. If possible, use a compactor to make sure it does. You can also ride over it gently with an ATV, which will press the seed firmly into the soil. By planting the seed just prior to a forecasted rainfall, you will greatly enhance germination.

For canola to have the best production, you will need to provide 200 to 300 lbs. of 19-19-19 per acre and 200 lbs. per acre of ammonium sulfate or 200 lbs. Per acre of 46-0-0 (urea). When a plot of canola is fertilized properly, it will provide about two tons of forage per acre!

Be sure to make the appropriate adjustments in the spreader for the size of the seed you are planting.

I have found that planting canola early is crucial to the plot's success. If rain is predicted, I plant it in early July or sometime soon thereafter. Canola needs 60 to 90 days to fully mature, so I never plant it any later than the first week in August because it will not mature if hit by frost before the 90-day period is up. By planting it in July, the canola should be up and running when the October bow season rolls around.

While I like to plant most of my plots as "pure plots," meaning only one type of seed, I have had success planting canola with other brassicas such as kale and rape. I always try to plant cold-weather clovers near my brassica plots to help divert the deer from over browsing them before November. This plan has saved several of my kale, rape, canola, turnip and sugar beet plots from being over eaten by deer. They prefer the sweet, tender Kura clover and birdsfoot trefoil from May to September—especially when those crops have been maintained well with fertilizer and cuttings.

You will be pleasantly shocked to see how often deer eat canola from November through January. A canola plot will help bring and hold deer on your property during the time you want them there—deer season! Give canola a try. You won't regret it.

One last word: Canola seed is hard to locate, but I found a reliable firm called Elk Mound Seed Company that carries it. Look for them on the Internet and check out their offerings.

# KURA CLOVER

Kura is a spreading, perennial clover that is one of the honeybees' most sought-after plants. It is winter hardy and will stand up to extreme cold-weather conditions. It can also tolerate severe, heavy grazing, making it an ideal nurse crop when you're planting small food plots.

Kura has an extensive root system and is more tolerant of drought than most other clovers which makes it perfect to plant in more arid locations. It has an upright stem that blooms with a large, whitish-pink flower in the spring. Its leaves, which are larger than other clovers and more pointed, have distinctive white, V-shaped markings.

As an extremely high-yielding, winter-hardy clover, Kura will not only survive, it will thrive. It withstands severe northern winters that are common on my farm in Otsego, NY, when other legumes don't. It will even outlast the other so-called cold-hardy clovers. The only down side to Kura clover is that it establishes slowly. Once it gets going, however, stands can last for many years.

Kura clover is an easy-to-grow plant that deer, turkey, and other wildlife forage on.

Kura can tolerate a pH range from 6.0 to 7.5, but it prefers a higher pH level rather than a lower one. Like other clovers and legumes, Kura must be inoculated with the correct Rhizobium strain— Trifolium Spec 3—before planting in a firm seed bed.

When planting Kura, make sure to get good seed-to-soil contact. It should be planted no deeper than one-quarter to one-half inch deep. If you plant Kura by itself, plant eight to 12 lbs. per acre. (Once again, see the section on forage rape to determine how much seed and fertilizer are required if you're planting a small plot.)

Kura can be planted in April or May, or it can be planted in late July or early August. It is much like alfalfa with regard to growth, production, and quality, but it is a lot easier to grow and manage, and once it gets established, it is sturdier than alfalfa.

Kura is my first choice when it comes to planting a pure stand of clover as well as when I'm planting other seeds that need a nurse crop to distract deer. It can also be mixed with birdsfoot trefoil, which is another extremely winter-hardy legume that is able to withstand severe winter temperatures. When planted by themselves or together, Kura and birdsfoot trefoil provide not only quality tonnage but also high levels of protein for your deer herd. They are top choices if you want to attract and hold deer from November through January.

## TO SUM IT UP ...

These are the plantings that will keep deer on your land during the important hunting months of October through December. Add something different from what is "typically" planted—and you will increase your hunting success!

# 30

# IMPROVE YOUR DEER SIGHTINGS BY 100 PERCENT

I first developed this strategy totally by accident in 1964 (my first year of hunting), while hunting deer on International Paper Company property in the Adirondack Mountains of New York. On a scouting trip during the weekend, I built a ground blind not far from where two main deer runways intersected, and where I saw a really nice buck with his nose held to the ground as he trotted along the trail looking for receptive does.

After building the blind, I mentally marked several nearby land-marks and headed out of the woods. I didn't want to use any type of markers for fear they would be seen by another hunter who would then find my ground blind and hunt from it.

On opening morning, I headed into the woods and was having trouble locating my blind. I knew I was close but, in the dark, I just couldn't see it. To stop making any more noise from crunching leaves and twigs, I waited in place until first light. At the first inkling of dawn, I was able to see the blind only 40 yards to my right, so I turned and slowly headed in that direction. About halfway there, I stepped on a twig and it snapped louder than a snapping turtle's mouth slamming shut. I froze in place—but not before I heard a series of snorts and saw "my" buck bolt for cover!

Totally frustrated about losing an opportunity to take a buck, I sat in the blind watching for deer, hoping the buck would return. I also thought of what I should do to avoid losing my way to the stand and, more importantly, get to it without making noise. Then I had an epiphany. I would rake a trail from a known point all the way to the stand, removing all leaves and other forest debris, (dead twigs and branches), no matter how long the trail might be. I knew that other hunters would probably see the raked trail, but if I got there before anyone else (and my raked trail theory worked) it would be worth the risk.

By 10 a.m. I was in the hardware store in Tupper Lake, some 30 miles from where I was hunting in Childwold. I picked up a heavy-duty leaf rake, and by 11:30, I was raking the trail. I finished up around 1:30 p.m. and went out to lunch. By 2:45, I was quietly making my way along my newly developed route. Once at the blind, I settled in and, not five minutes later, I heard the unmistakable sounds of a deer's hooves crunching leaves. Within moments a six-point buck ambled down the deer trail. I put the scope on him and squeezed off a shot. To my total amazement, the buck jumped and ran off into the surrounding cover. In my excitement (remember, this was my first year of deer hunting), I had missed him cleanly!

It didn't matter. I had just come up with my very first deer-hunting strategy, and as far as I was concerned, it was totally responsible for getting me to my stand without making noise to spook the buck that was obviously close to my blind when I entered it. That was all I needed. From that day on, I was absolutely hooked and believed in the benefits of raking a deer trail to my hunting stand. For the next several years, this one tactic proved to be the primary reason I took several excellent bucks in New York—especially in the Catskill region.

Over the last 45 years, raking trails has helped me sneak quietly into places where deer feed, bed, hold over in—even into buck core areas. I have done so without the unavoidable crunching of leaves or the inadvertent snapping of an unseen twig or dead branch. This is especially true in the darkness of pre-dawn light and, surprisingly, when hunting off-hours between 10 a.m. and 2 p.m. This one tactic has improved my sightings of deer tenfold and has helped me kill bucks and does that I would have otherwise spooked long before I saw them.

My tactic has undergone some technological changes over the years. I now use a heavy-duty leaf blower to remove most, if not all, of the leaves, and I only use the rake to remove stubborn wet leaves and other remaining forest debris. I also carry a heavy-duty pruner called the E-Z Kut Ratchet Pruner (www.woodyhunting.com) that I use to cut away any annoying branches hanging over the raked trail. In low-light conditions, these branches can rub on your clothing and make noise or, more importantly, their sharp thorn branches could stick you in the face or eye in the dark. This pruner also comes in handy to cut those really aggravating tree roots that seem to reach out and grab your foot as you walk along, sending you tumbling to the ground. So over the years, I have added some tools to improve my strategy.

Some of the other benefits of raking trails to your stands are worth mentioning. How many times have you gone to a stand that you are familiar with only to discover that it seems to have disappeared? (Most of us immediately get the sinking feeling that it was stolen.) You walk in circles looking for it and eventually find it. But not before you have crunched leaves or frozen snow, or snapped a twig or two.

Not only have you made additional noise trying to find the stand, you have also wasted valuable hunting time. Add to the equation that if the stand is on a mountainside or in thick cover, you begin to sweat up a storm as you move more and more quickly looking for it. All elements combined can lead up to a bad morning of hunting.

By taking the time to rake a trail to your deer stand, you eliminate the possibility of "losing" that stand. On one occasion, I raked a trail that went by one stand and ended at another. I had intended to hunt the first stand, went right by it in the darkness and ended up having to hunt from the second stand. As it turned out, I didn't see a deer that morning. What I should have done was walk quickly and quietly back to the first stand. With the raked trail, I wouldn't have made any noise—just lost some time.

Deer also use the raked trails even if they weren't using them before, and their tracks can now show you their travel patterns! Time and time again I have noticed that soon after raking a trail to my stand, deer begin to walk along it. Sometimes they start using the trail as quickly as a half-a-day later and will walk along it for quite some distance. Sometimes they eventually go off the trail; other times they take it to the end.

One year, my cousin, Leo, and I raked a trail on my farm only a day before hunting season began so that my wife, Kate, could make a quiet approach to her stand. The next morning, her shot rang out loud and clear only moments after legal shooting light. While we dragged the deer out, we noticed, (but were not surprised to find) that the trail was covered in deer tracks and littered with deer dung. It took the deer only one day to figure out the trail offered a much quieter approach from the hayfields to their bedding area.

As noted in the incident above, as soon as one deer uses the trail, others will quickly follow. I have discovered that when I rake trails in thick, over grown areas where bucks like to hang out, the deer will use the raked trail rather than their deer trail. I don't know exactly why they do this, but it could be because they realize a raked trail is quieter to walk along or that the trail provides a path of least resistance, which all deer naturally want to use. Either way, they like using raked trails and most of my stands are set up along them.

By leaf blowing or hand raking dry leaves and other forest debris along trails leading to hunting blinds, you'll cut the chance of alerting deer as you approach by 75 percent or more resulting in more deer sightings and shooting opportunities.

Of course, there are some downsides to raking trails: they take work and time. On some occasions they will freeze and make just as much noise (or more) than an unraked trail. But that is rare and doesn't happen enough for me not to use the strategy.

If you hunt public ground, raked trails can and will lead other hunters to your area; unless you are like me and hang a lot of blaze

## TOOLS THAT MAKE RAKING TRAILS EASY

- A powerful, gas-operated leaf blower
- A heavy-duty leaf rake
- A pair of E-Z Kut Pruners
- A pair of leather work gloves (to prevent blisters when raking)
- A fanny pack with water and snacks (because you'll be a long time)

orange ribbons off the trail as a decoy to lead other hunters away from your stand. Then hunters assume that you're really hunting where the ribbons are and head that way instead! Raked trails also dampen the sound of approaching deer to the point that most deer walking along a raked trail, seem to magically appear . . . without any warning at all. Therefore, hunters must be alert for any sign of movement and must listen for the slightest sounds, or they will miss opportunities when deer pass by.

Not surprisingly, raked trails work best on land you own or lease. You will discover that, once you try this tactic, it will be one of the most effective strategies you can use to get to your stand quickly and quietly. It can also help a hunter get quietly to the edge of the woods that look over a food plot, apple orchard, corn or soybean field, or other area that is difficult to sneak up on—places where deer will hear and see you long before you get close.

The effort of raking deer trails has been worth its weight in gold several times over for me through the years. The key is to think that no trail is too long to rake or isn't worth the time. Raking trails will improve your sightings and your bag limit the very first season you make them. Give it a try this season and you, too, will discover it is one "hot" commodity!

# 31

# HOW TO BUILD A FALSE RUB TO ATTRACT BUCKS

Many years ago, I accidentally discovered how making a fake buck rub on a tree can attract both resident and transient bucks post-haste—especially during the big chase period.

It happened in early November of 1986, when I discovered the haunts of a solid 135-class 10-point buck. I was hunting on public ground, so other hunters were using the area as well. Every morning, two noisy bowhunters would tramp down the trail, talking and cracking limbs, as they walked to their respective stands. I could hear them coming from the moment they slammed the truck door until they passed my location.

One morning, they actually arrived earlier than I and one of them caught sight of me as I was leaving the main trail and moving into the woods. They must have thought that's where my stand was located. (Actually, I had stopped to pee.)

It was my third year as host of my television show, "Woods n' Water," and I was viewed as something of a local celebrity at the time—which often meant added competition in the places I hunted. The two nodded and continued on their way, but not before mentioning that they had seen "some good bucks" in the area I was heading to. They had been planning on hunting that area, they said, but would go someplace else that day.

I knew they were fibbing because my spot was another 200 yards down the trail. The times they has been in the woods when I was, I'd heard them walk past me and continue along for at least 100 yards before I couldn't hear them anymore. I had to come up with a game plan that would prevent those guys from finding my spot.

That night, I fell asleep thinking about how I could distract them into hunting another spot long before they got near my stand. Then a light went on! Since I hunted off the left side of the trail, I would make a big rub on the right side, along with several smaller rubs that would make a rub line about 75 yards long. I decided to put the first rub right off the trail and at least 200 yards before the spot where I had entered the woods.

I made the rubs the next day during a time when I knew the two hunters had left the woods, and I must admit those rubs were impressive and realistic looking. The next morning, I waited along the trail hidden in some brush. As the duo came down the trail, I saw them stop and heard them get all excited about the first rub. When they spotted the second rub, which was about 30 yards from the first, one of them instantly took off in that direction. The other quickly walked back the way he'd come, and I suspect he set up not far away as well. I almost laughed out loud, and it took all my willpower to hold it in.

"What a freakin' genius I am," I whispered to myself, and then quickly made my way to my stand.

I didn't see the buck that morning, so about 10 a.m. I decided I'd go get some coffee and return to hunt around 1 p.m. I was walking down the trail when my heart skipped a beat. There on the trail were the bow hunters, resting. Attached to a deer drag was "my" 10-point buck!

The first knucklehead spoke to me—and I am paraphrasing here, but until this day I remember most of what he said:

"How the hell did a guy like you miss those rubs along the trail this morning? You're supposed to be a big deer hunter—you must have come in half asleep! We almost didn't go out this morning. I'm glad we did, though, because on the way in I spotted a really fresh rub off the trail that led to a rub line and I set up about 50 yards off the trail, figuring the buck that made them would show up again. About

9 a.m. this bad boy came walking in, freshening up each rub as he passed it. When he got to my rub, I drew back and let 'er fly."

The second knucklehead then chimed in, "Not a bad morning's hunt—huh?"

"No, not at all," I said. Then I congratulated Mr. Knucklehead and offered to help them drag the buck out—which, thankfully, they declined.

I continued cursing myself out with cuss words that hadn't been invented yet, asking myself one important question: *"Who's really the knucklehead, knucklehead?"*

On the drive home, (note: I didn't have the ambition to return to the area to go hunting that afternoon), it finally hit me. The false rubs had actually attracted that buck! *"You jerk,"* I thought. (I don't want to repeat what I really called myself.) *"You created an ass-kicking, buck-killing tactic that worked for the guys you were trying to deceive! How's that for turn-around-is-fair-play,"* I mused. Oh well, as the old adage goes, "payback is a bitch."

From that day on, I swore I would share each and every tactic I ever created, used, thought of, or read about with any and all deer hunters who cared to listen. Now, are you ready to learn how to use this mock-rub tactic to bag your next buck? You should be.

I have been using this tactic successfully since 1986. While, like other deer hunting strategies I use, it doesn't work every time, it works enough times to make it worthwhile.

## RUBS: VISUAL & OLFACTORY SIGNPOSTS

Let's take a serious look at what a rub actually means to a buck. Most hunters know a rub can indicate a buck's travel route. Let's say you're hunting near the top of a ridge and above you is the bedding area. Below you are feeding sources like corn or soybean fields, apple orchards, acorn crops, etc. While you are walking up to the ridge, you spot a rub facing you. If you walk beyond that rub, turn around, face down the ridge and look carefully about 30 to 50 yards to either side of the rub you first found, you will see more rubs facing you.

You have just discovered the morning and evening travel routes of a buck moving between his bedding and feeding areas. This may seem insignificant, but the sign helps hunters to set up a stand based on the time of day or evening that the buck is actually using one trail or the other. So you now can maximize your time afield by not hunting a spot that a buck will not be using that time of the day.

This is just a minor point when it comes to rubs. A rub is a very important social signpost to both the local bucks and, equally important, to transient bucks who enter areas outside their home turf. Rubs are used by ALL bucks that come from the same area to express their social status and current rutting condition.

A buck rub is a visual and olfactory sign post to other deer. By depositing several of his individual odors against the bark of the tree his is leaving a very specific message. The combination of odors tell other deer exactly who the buck was, how long ago he visited the rub, how old he is and the status of his present rut condition is. (photo courtesy Ted Rose)

Despite what some hunters think, within a given herd there is not a single dominant buck. *Dominance* (in the true sense of the word) is not part of the white-tailed deer's behavior. The term is only used to hype products and get hunters to believe that certain deer scents, calls, and other gimmicks should be used if they want to kill a "dominant buck." This often leads some veteran hunters and a lot of novices down a path that distorts the real facts about whitetail behavior.

Real *dominance* is seen in the large cats and canines of Africa; wolves and coyotes of North America, and other animals that specifically delineate a territorial boundary. They use urine to warn others of their species not to trespass. If the area is infringed upon, the interloper will find itself in a fight for its very life.

Whitetails simply don't fight to the death when transient bucks enter their territory. Nor do they protect a specific area with urine to warn other bucks away. Therefore, dominance is not part of the white- tail's lifestyle—at least, not as it is hyped.

Every buck within a given herd knows his place in the pecking order long before the rut. While they are in velvet, bucks use body language to establish what step of the ladder each occupies in their world. That way, by the time the rut comes around they are able to avoid serious fights that could injure or possibly even kill them. It is very rare for bucks to kill each other unless the buck-to-doe population is seriously out of kilter and there are many more bucks than does. This simply doesn't happen often in the wild.

An individual buck uses a wide variety of visual, aural, and olfactory signs to communicate (and I use that word loosely) with other bucks and does in his territory, including his glands, saliva, urine, defecation, antlers, body language, vocalizations, body size and position in the pecking order. Each gland releases specific odors that "say" to another buck, "Hey I'm Joe. Any other buck smelling this rub (or scrape, urine, scat, etc.) will detect by these odors that I rank among the top of the pecking order."

Each and every buck that approaches an existing rub, or is ready to make a fresh rub, does the exact same things each time: he either approaches the existing rub or the tree he is about to make a rub on or stops about five feet from it.

Then the buck squats and urinates.

While urinating, the buck squats slightly further down, putting (I believe) added pressure on a gland in the penis called the *pre-pucial* gland. The secretions from the gland help to lubricate the penal sheath and release pheromones that tell other bucks and does the status of the buck's present rutting condition. This is an important part of the rubbing sequence.

Next, the buck approaches the rub or the tree he is about to rub and he sniffs it carefully several times before doing anything else.

The buck then licks the rub, or the back of the tree he is about to rub, several times in order to deposit scent from a gland called the *vomeronasal organ*, located in the roof of his mouth. This organ is used primarily to analyze the status of an estrus doe as her urine scent flows past it when the buck lip curls (called the *flehmen gesture*). It is also used to analyze the rut status of other bucks.

When making a rub, however, the buck is leaving scent from his vomeronasal organ to express his current rutting status. At the same time, he is leaving scent from his salivary glands. These glands contain enzymes that primarily aid in the digestion of foods. When saliva is deposited on a rub, the enzymes also let other bucks in his herd know exactly which buck left it and his exact rutting status. A buck will also leave saliva on overhanging branches above a scrape that he is making or one that he may be refreshing that was made by another buck. (Yes, bucks do use scrapes of other bucks and some does will, too). A buck will use the same saliva scent when making or refreshing a licking stick as well.

His next move will be to rub his forehead glands (located between the top of the eyes and the antlers) on the tree. These glands, which are most active during the rut, are vitally important when deer rub trees. Biologists have substantiated that there is a correlation between the buck's age, social status (his position in the pecking order), and these glands. They seem to be most pungent and active in mature, high-ranking bucks. (Note: I did not use the "D" word—*dominant*) The glands produce an oily substance that makes the hair around them dark and, in some cases, black. When the buck is rubbing a tree, the oil is transferred to the rub. It is also deposited on overhanging branches. Some experts believe that the scent from the forehead gland also helps to attract does to a buck's rub or scrape. I can tell you this for sure: I know when I make a fake rub and use real or synthetic forehead gland scent, I will often see does visit the rub.

I cannot overemphasize that all the scents a buck deposits on the rub, in a scrape, or on an overhanging branch help to announce his social status and current rut condition to other bucks within his herd and even to the "dreaded" transient buck.

If you are still unsure that making a mock rub will work, consider this point: Deer survive within their daily environment (especially during the hunting season) not through the power of intelligence, or accumulated learning abilities stored to memory. They survive entirely by their keen instinctive and olfactory abilities. Period. End of story. A deer comes to a call not because it understands anything else, but because its instinct tells it that the sound is coming from another deer. It investigates a decoy not because the brain says, "Hey, that is a deer I just have to check out," but rather because its instinct forces it to investigate it . . . if all else is right with its nose.

Deer react to visual stimulation much more than hunters like to believe, and will often be instinctively forced to investigate something when they really shouldn't. Therefore, a mock rub acts on this instinctive behavior. The buck is drawn to it because his instinct tells him that it is natural and should be immediately investigated. When a buck-be it a spike or trophy-class animal-sees a freshly made rub, it has no choice but to investigate it. All its natural instincts are telling it how to behave, as long as it doesn't pick up any danger signal (like human odor) while doing so.

Not many tactics work on so many of a deer's instincts at one time as a false rub does. The buck can see the highly visual object from quite a distance as he meanders through the area, and he instantly recognizes it as a signpost to deposit his scent and calling card in order to communicate his presence and status to other bucks. This fresh, new rub demands the buck's attention. Instinctively, he thinks it was made by another competitive buck—one that is, perhaps, still in the area making rubs and scrapes.

In addition, as I mentioned above, the rub will contain a combination of odors that the buck can detect from a distance as well— sometimes long before he even sees the rub. Again, these olfactory cues play on the buck's instincts to check the rub out as soon as possible.

By now you're saying, "Alright already—tell me how I make a false rub!" So, ok. Here we go:

The key to making a false rub is to find a natural rub that was made recently (earlier that season). Then go about 30 to 50 yards from it and select a tree that is similar in circumference and height to make your mock rub. Why? Well, that is going to take a bit of explaining. Your mock rub must look and smell natural to attract a buck—that is the fact of the matter. It must NOT suggest to a buck, no matter how large its antlers are, that the rub was made by a bigger, more aggressive buck within the area. (Please note: once again, I did not use the "D" word.)

As I have said, bucks establish the pecking order within their herd long before they shed the velvet from their antlers. They know who is sitting at the top of the social ladder and who is on the lowest rung. Pushing and shoving matches and even some more serious fighting only occur between rivals in the group that are closely matched in body weight, antler size, and age. Therefore, a two-and-a-half-year-old buck will seldom pick a fight with a four-and-a-half-year-old or older buck—especially one he knows from his group. Instinct tells him the fight is hopeless and he avoids the conflict instead of risking injury.

I often tell people at my seminars that if they want to use deer calls, they should NOT use them loudly or aggressively. It just isn't natural. Hunters who use calls that are sold as "dominant" or "aggressive" grunts, snort wheezes, or barks and roars are kidding themselves and are being sold a bunch of hype.

What? You don't agree? Then ask yourself these questions: In all the years that you have hunted, isn't it true that 99.999999 percent of the grunts you have heard are low, guttural sounds? Did you ever hear a roar, or a bark, or a loud, piercing grunt? I'm going to bet that you probably haven't. And for those of you who think you have, consider this: If such loud, aggressive barks, roars, and overly audible grunts were made by bucks, then all of us would be hearing them throughout the woods. However, we're not, are we? Instead, an overwhelming majority of the grunts detected by hunters are barely audible until the buck is close by. Even then, they can be so low-pitched that a hunter may miss them.

The fact is that a buck will avoid another aggressive buck about 95 percent of the time. Most potential "fights" are simply and quickly settled with aggressive displays of body language. If you want to be consistently successful when using deer calls, rattling antlers or decoys, don't try to be the biggest bad-boy on the block. Instead, make sounds that other bucks instinctively find attractive because they hear them as "beatable" opponents.

Still having trouble believing what I'm saying? Then follow this analogy: I grew up boxing. I boxed in the Police Athlete League (PAL) in the army and in more than my share of street fights in Brooklyn, New York. I can take care of myself when it comes to using my fists. But under normal conditions, I wouldn't fight with someone who is bigger, appears stronger, or displays more aggressive body language.

Why? Survival instinct dictates that I avoid the fight. So I show some sign to the larger, more aggressive opponent that I want to back off. I dart my eyes toward the ground or make some other physical gesture that indicates I'm looking for a way out of the fight. In other words, I acknowledge his strength and communicate that I'm not looking to get a butt whipping—a message I want to send quickly and clearly to my would-be opponent. If he doesn't back off, then my "fight or flight" response kicks in. In most cases when facing a larger, more physically fit opponent, people and animals will choose the latter.

A rub gives off signals in much the same way. Its mere presence (and odor) tells another buck about the potential size and status of the buck that made it. Therefore, when a buck sees a rub that is substantially larger than the surrounding rubs, he is immediately put off by its size and becomes instantly cautious. He will avoid it rather than approach it. Trust me on this point.

Rubs on large diameter trees are often rubbed by several different bucks of different ages. The gouge mark at the top left suggests at least one buck had a full rack with long tines, one of which probably made the deep gouge.

When creating mock-rub reduce human scent by wearing surgeon gloves and rubber boots. Make the fake rub within 30 yards of a natural rub. Allow the shavings to hang from the false rub.

To make a natural looking mock-rub—one that won't spook a deer's sense of smell or vision—you will need the following items:

- A bottle of pure buck urine

- A bottle of All-Season Deer Lure (a combination of hide and body odors of deer)

- A bottle of interdigital scent (although you will only use one single drop of it at the site of your mock rub)

- A bottle of forehead gland and tarsal scent (Buck Fever Synthetics makes a scent that combines both odors.)

You will also need a pair of thin latex gloves (like the ones doctors wear), and several large bore-cleaning patches (placed in a small plastic zip-top bag). Lastly, you will need a small, easy-to-carry tape measure, essential for helping you make your fake rub more realistic.

The soles of your boots (rubber or leather) should be clean and free of foreign odors. Wash them with non-scented soap the evening before making a mock rub and apply a drop of interdigital scent on each boot sole. Of course, your clothes and body should be as scent free as you can make them.

When you have located a natural rub, find another tree that is equal in circumference and height. Measure the natural rub from where it begins at the lower end of the tree to where it ends at the upper part. No matter what size it is, you should make your mock rub about three inches smaller. You don't want it to look like it was made by King-Kong, right? You want it to suggest it was made by a buck that is easily intimidated, which is the key to all calling, rattling and decoying tactics—yes?

Once you select a tree on which to make your mock-rub, use one small-to-average natural antler that has at least four tines on it. Begin to shred the bark with an aggressive up and down motion on the same side of the tree that the natural rub you found is showing. Make sure you don't remove any peeling bark. Let it hang or fall naturally while you are rubbing the antlers on the tree.

This process can be done with a small handsaw, as long as the saw's teeth are fine and not large. (A saw with large teeth will not scrape the bark away like a deer's antlers would, and the rub will look unnatural.) But I prefer to use a small natural shed antler (mine is probably 10 years old) because I feel it leaves a realistic look and still provides some type of bone scent on the rub as well.

Remember, do not rub all around the trunk of the tree—just one side. When you think your mock rub is finished, step back and see if it compares to the natural rub you are trying to duplicate. If so, go to the next step. (If not, get it right before going on.)

Take your antler (if you're using a saw to make the rub, you'll need a nail-punch to replace the tine of the antler) and press a single point of a tine into the trunk of the tree. Just create a small dent in a few places high and low within the rub and a few in the bark of the tree above the rub. This duplicates the penetration made by the tips of the tines on the rack of a buck (big or small) as he rubs a tree. As I have said about all my deer-hunting tactics, once you are committed to using the tactic, always make a concerted effort to create the ENTIRE illusion.

Add a tiny amount of forehead or preorbital scent on the tree. Then place a few drops of buck urine mixed with tarsal scent on the ground. By adding scent to your mock rub this will help "create the entire illusion."

Before doing anything else, measure the size of your rub and write it down on paper. Do not try to record the size to memory. I will explain why soon.

Now, take some forehead scent and place several drops onto a fresh bore-cleaning patch. Rub the patch and scent along the entire portion of the rub. Put a few drops of All-Season Deer Lure on another clean patch and dab it along the sides of the rub. At the base of the tree squirt several drops of pure buck urine and a SINGLE DROP of interdigital scent. Those of you who think more than one drop will work better will find out it won't—the hard way. (All deer avoid excess odors of interdigital.) Then put down a couple of drops of tarsal scent around the tree—two drops will do nicely; more won't.

Walk back from your mock rub about 10 yards and put down about 10 to 15 drops or a few good squirts worth of the straight buck urine on the forest floor. Make it spray in several directions, like a buck would—but not all over the place. A doe urinates in a single spot. A buck dangles while urinating. (You know what I mean. You don't always hit the bowl, do you?) "Create the entire illusion."

When you have completed your mock rub, waste no time in setting up your treestand or ground blind, and then wait. The first buck to happen through the area will see and smell the rub and he will have no freakin' choice but to instinctively head to it to check it out. Unless he catches wind of you, sees you or hears you, he will go toward the mock rub, stop, stare at it, smell the buck urine, and then urinate over it or close by it and move to the rub. He will go through all the traditional sniffing, licking, and rubbing motions to try and discover the buck that made the rub, and to let him know who made the new rub.

I want to be perfectly clear here. The tactic doesn't work all the time—but it does work often enough to be high on my list of strategies to use. My records also indicate the most successful dates for making false rubs are from October 31 through November 13. But I have had success with this tactic through the third week of November and, occasionally, during the post rut of December. Like all tactics, it has its moments of huge success and days of no response at all. You can use deer calls, like a soft grunt or an estrus doe blat, to bring a buck in to where he may see your mock rub. Rattling also works, but not as often as deer calls do.

But no matter what you decide to use: just an ambush, deer calls, rattling, or a combination, when this strategy works your heart will pound out of your chest, I promise you that!

After two or three days of not seeing a buck, it is time to reevaluate the spot. Here is where your tape measure comes in and the measurement you jotted down on paper. (You did jot it down, right?) After three days without anything happening, measure your rub. If it is the same length you made it—what was that number again? Wait, let me check my paper . . . oh 13 1/2 inches—and it is still that size, it is time to move on and try the tactic someplace else. It will eventually work.

If your 13 1/2-inch rub has turned into 15 1/2 inches, you will know without question that the rub was indeed visited—but just not when you were there. You can spend another day over it (I would hunt it from 10 a.m. to 2 p.m. if you have been hunting it in the mornings and evenings). If it doesn't produce then, move on to another location at least 200 yards away.

While this tactic has proven to work best by creating all the elements I mentioned above, you could improvise if need be. I have made mock rubs when I came across a really large, fresh rub and made them with nothing more than my handsaw and some buck urine, and I have had reasonable response.

So there you have it—one of my better and more successful strategies.

After making a mock rub, measure the exact length and write it down. The next time you hunt near the rub, measure it again. If it is larger, a buck visited your mock rub when you weren't there. A trail camera will provide the exact time the buck visited the rub - don't be surprised if it was between 10 am and 1 pm!

# 32

# STEP-BY-STEP FIELD DRESSING

In order to ensure the most flavorful-tasting meat, it is essential that you know how to field dress game quickly and efficiently. By following the instructions and tips in this DIY section, you will get the most from your harvested big game, ensuring the elimination of any "gamey" flavor. There is no doubt that knowing how to properly field dress a big buck is the most important element to having quality, terrific-tasting game meat.

Before the advent of the most helpful of field-dressing tools, Hunter's Specialties Butt Out®, one of the most crucial steps was the process of removing the anal tract and bladder. It must be done without puncturing either the tract or the bladder, which would lead to unwanted spillage within the body cavity. Fluids leaking into the body cavity are prime causes of either poor-tasting game meat or, worse yet, contaminated meat.

Even though it can be a difficult and undesirable task, cutting around and removing the anal canal on deer is an unavoidable and necessary step in field dressing. With the Butt-Out big-game field-dressing tool, however, hunters can quickly and easily remove the anal-alimentary canal on deer and deer-sized game.

## STEP # 1

Place the deer on as flat a surface as possible, keeping the head slightly higher than the rest of the body. By doing this, gravity will help the entrails slide out of the body cavity more easily when they are cut free.

## STEP # 2

Remove the anal tract by inserting the Butt-Out all the way into the deer's anal cavity and pushing it in as far as you can (all the way to the end of the tool's handle). Next, slowly turn the tool until you feel it "catch." Then, slowly and steadily pull the tool out until you have about a 10-inch section of the deer's intestine outside of the body cavity. Almost the entire section will be filled with deer pellets (dung). Where the pellets end, the anal tract will appear white. This is where you can cut off the tract and lay it aside. Now, the rest of the field- dressing process will be accomplished much more quickly and effectively.

The Butt-Out tool makes the task of field dressing quicker and much easier. I'd rather forget my pee-bottle home than my Butt Out tool! (photo courtesy Hunter's Specialties)

While slowly removing a Butt-Out tool, apply slow, steady movement and motion. Do not quickly pull, jerk, or yank out the tool. (photo courtesy Hunter's Specialties)

# STEP # 3

Turn the deer on its back. Make a shallow 2- to 3-inch cut on the side of the penis, or on the udder if you are field dressing a doe. Separate the external reproductive organs of a buck from the abdominal wall. If it is a doe, remove the udder. Milk sours quickly in the udder, causes a foul smell, and gives the meat a very disagreeable taste. Check local game laws before removing the genitals because some states require that they remain attached to the carcass. If it's legal to remove them, however, carefully cut them free of the skin and let them hang over the back of the anus. It is important not to cut them free of the viscera at this point.

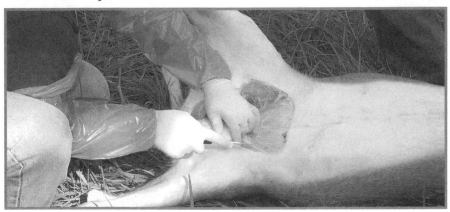

Once the anal tract is totally removed, make a shallow cut to open up the abdominal wall. Depending upon the local game laws, you may need to leave the sex organs attached. (photo courtesy Hunter's Specialties)

## STEP # 4

Straddle the deer while you are facing its head. Pinch a piece of skin and pull it up and away from the body. Insert the tip of the knife blade and make a very shallow slit into the muscle and skin, which will prevent accidentally puncturing the intestines. Make the cut just long enough to insert the first two fingers.

Now form a "V" with your with your index and first fingers and very carefully continue to slit a thin layer of abdominal muscle and skin all the way up to the sternum of the rib cage. As you make this cut, the intestines and stomach will begin to push out from the body cavity, but will not fall entirely free, as they will still be attached by connective tissue.

When opening up the rest of the body cavity, use your fingers (pointer and index fingers) in the shape of a "V" as a guide for your knife. As with all field dressing and butchering jobs, make sure your knife is sharp before you begin. (photo courtesy Hunter's Specialties)

## STEP # 5

If you are not going to mount the deer's head, the next step is to make a cut through the rib cage. While straddling the deer, slightly bend your knees, face the head and, with the knife blade facing up, position it under the breastbone. Using both your hands, placed over each other and around the handle of the knife for leverage, cut through the cartilage in the center of the breastbone and continue cutting up through the neck. If you intend to mount the deer's head, stop at the brisket line and skip steps 5 and 6.

## STEP # 6

Once the neck is open, free the windpipe and esophagus by cutting the connective tissue. Grasp them firmly and pull them down toward the body cavity while continuing to cut any connective tissues as you proceed.

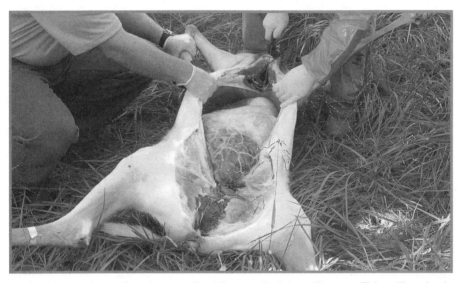

In the above photo, the chest cavity (ribs section) is split open. This will make is easier to remove the windpipe and lungs. But, if you will be mounting the head, you must not cut the hide beyond the rib cage. (photo courtesy Hunter's Specialties)

## STEP # 7

If you are going to mount the deer's head, you will have to tie off the gullet (throat), push it forward as far as possible and cut it free from the windpipe. Also cut around the diaphragm and remove the connective tissue of the lungs and other organs. Then carefully reach up as far as you can into the throat area—as high as your arms will take you—to sever the esophagus and trachea. Be aware of where your knife blade is, as most knife accidents occur during this step because you can't see what you're cutting.

## STEP # 8

If you haven't already removed the rectum with a Butt-Out tool, it is at this point you will have to address that job. Some hunters prefer

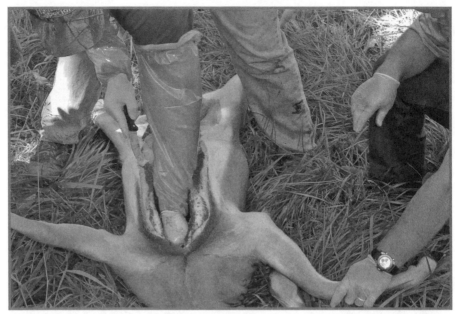

Be sure to carry elbow-length gloves in your backpack. They help to stop blood, ticks, and fleas from getting on your clothes. Make sure the gloves are tight-fitting on your hands. This will help you "feel around" better when making cuts. (photo courtesy Hunter's Specialties)

to remove the rectal tract and urethra by slicing between the hams or splitting the pelvic bone, whether they are field dressing a buck or a doe. Others remove the anal tract first by placing the point of a knife to the side of the rectum and making a cut that completely encircles the rectum.

Position the tip of the blade into the pelvic area and cut around the entire anus. Free the rectum and urethra by loosening the connective tissue with the tip of the knife blade. To prevent any leakage from the anal tract and the urethra, tie them off with a stout piece of string. Next comes the tricky part of the whole process: Push the tied-off rectum and urethra under the pelvic bone and into the body cavity. If you choose, you may split the pelvic bone, which makes removing the rectum and urethra easier—but it requires using a stout knife or small axe.

## STEP # 9

Grasp one side of the rib cage firmly with one hand and pull it open. Cut all remaining connective tissue along the diaphragm free from the rib opening down to the backbone, staying as close to the rib cage as possible. Be careful not to puncture the stomach, intestines, or any other internal matter. Now, repeat the same procedure on the other side so both cuts meet over the backbone.

Reach up and grasp the windpipe and esophagus and pull them down and away from the body cavity. Detach the heart and liver. Now all innards should be free of any connective tissue, which will allow you to scoop all remaining entrails out onto the ground, along with as much blood as possible from the body cavity.

## STEP # 10

Once all the entrails have been removed from the deer's body cavity, it is important to cool it as quickly as possible. Prop the body cavity open with a stick or a very handy tool called Rib-Cage Spreader made by Outdoor Edge.

If at all possible, wash out the body cavity with water or snow to rid it of any dirt, debris, excess blood, etc. Hanging the deer as soon as possible will greatly enhance the cooling process. If hanging isn't possible, turn it over—open cavity down—and let it drain any remaining blood or fluids.

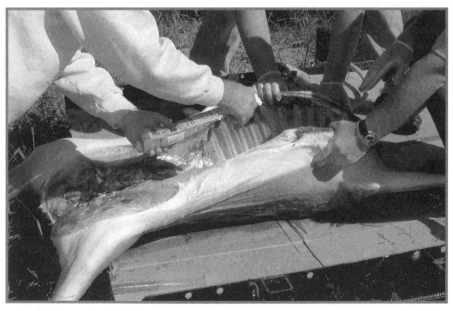

Once the body cavity is free from all the entrails, flush it out with water to get rid of any remaining blood or entrails. This will help reduce the amount of bacterial growth on the inside of the carcass. (photo courtesy Hunter's Specialties)

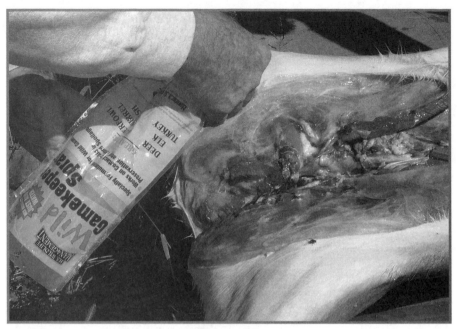

The exposed meat of this deer is being sprayed with Gamekeeper Spray. This spray helps reduce the amount of spoilage of the exposed meat. (photo courtesy Hunter's Specialties)

## DID YOU KNOW . . . ?

• There is no real benefit in cutting a deer's throat to "bleed-it-out."

• A small knife with a 3- to 5-inch blade is the ideal size knife to use when field dressing a deer.

• Cooling your deer as soon as possible will help retain the overall flavor of the meat.

• To "age" deer meat properly, it must be kept at temperatures between 38 and 42 degrees. Hanging a deer in a tree to "age" for days, or even longer periods of time, only decays the meat and makes it much less flavorful and tender.

# 33

# HOW TO SKIN A DEER IN 6 STEPS

Once your deer is field dressed, it's important that you remove the hide as quickly as possible in order to cool the meat down. Skinning a deer right after it has been field dressed will help provide you with better-tasting venison. This chapter will show you how to skin a deer using only a sharp knife, sharpening steel, small saw, gambrel and deer hoist—all the tools needed to make this task go smoothly.

## STEP # 1

Peel the deer's skin (and hide) over the hind leg to reveal the large tendon located at the back of the leg. Carefully slit any connective tissue between the bone and the large tendon. Next, place the end of the gambrel between the leg bone and the tendon (see photo next page). Now, hoist the carcass to a height at which it is comfortable to work.

To make the job of skinning easier, hang the deer at a comfortable working height for you. The task will go more quickly and with less strain on your back, and neck if you don't have to repeatedly reach up or bend down while removing the hide. (photo CPi)

Once the hide is cut free from the inner side of each leg, pull it around the leg as shown. Most times you can pull long sections of the hide away quite freely. Other times, use the tip of your knife to cut it away from the muscle. (photo CPi)

# STEP # 2

With the knife blade turned away from the carcass, cut the hind quarter along the inner side of each leg. Turn the knife blade back toward the meat and begin skinning the hide around the leg. Pull hard on the hide with your hands once you reach the outside of each leg.

# STEP # 3

Using a firm grip, pull the remaining hide down the outside of each leg until the skinned part reaches the deer's tail. Separate the tail as close to the deer's rump as possible, being careful not to cut into the meat. The tail should remain inside or attached to the hide. Continue skinning the hide along the deer's back by pulling it in a downward motion with your hand while at the same time slicing it free as close to the meat of the body with your knife.

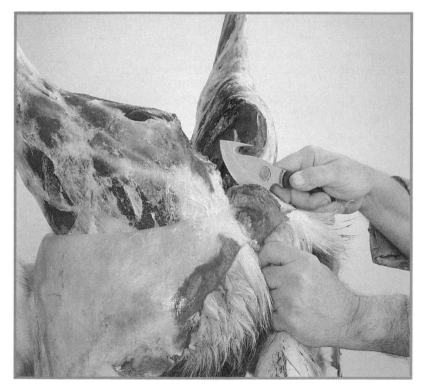

To remove the tail, skin under and around it and then peel the hide over the tail about an inch or so. Use either a sharp skinning knife or saw to cut it off close to the body. (photo CPi)

# STEP # 4

Once you reach the middle of the deer's torso, grip the hide with both hands and continue to pull it down. Use the tip of your knife blade only to free the hide in places where it hangs up. Be extra careful not to slice into or cut off pieces of meat still attached to the hide. Also, be careful not to cut holes in the hide while using the tip of the knife blade. Using your hands, continue to peel the hide down the deer's back and around the rib cage until you reach the shoulders.

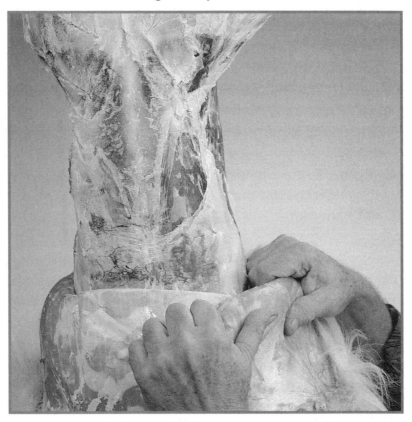

Before you begin pulling the hide down the middle of the deer's torso, adjust the height of the deer so that you have maximum leverage when you pull. (photo CPi)

# STEP # 5

At this point, cut along the inside of each of the front legs with your knife and peel the hide off the legs. With a stout knife or butcher saw, remove the front legs just above the first joint (located slightly above the deer's hooves).

To make skinning easy, at this point, cut off the deer's front legs just above the first joint. Note: Some hunters prefer to remove the legs before removing the hide. Either way works. (photo CPi)

## STEP # 6

Keep pulling, cutting, and peeling the hide as far down the deer's neck as possible. When you've worked the hide to the lowest point on the neck, cut off the deer's head using your saw. Once the hide is removed from the deer, spread it out on a clean, flat surface with the hair facing down and scrape off any remaining pieces of fat, tallow, meat, and blood. The hide is now ready to be salted if it is going to be preserved.

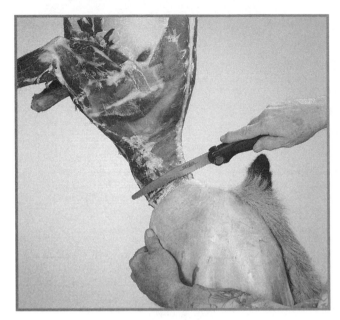

When it comes time to remove the deer's head, make sure you have a razor-sharp knife and sturdy saw at hand. It will make the job quicker and easier. (photo CPi)

### DID YOU KNOW...?

• It is much easier to skin a deer or other game animal while the hide is still warm.

• To make the job of skinning go more quickly, hang the deer by a pulley so you can raise or lower it to eye level without straining your arms and back—and avoid getting a back and/or neck ache.

• To keep the deer's hair off the meat, cut through the skin from the inside out. By skinning the hide in this manner, your knife will slip between the hairs instead of slicing them in half and getting them all over the meat. It will also prevent your knife from dulling as quickly.

• To avoid mistakenly removing pieces of meat, use as sharp a knife as possible while skinning the hide from the deer. Remember to use your sharpening steel to touch up the knife blade repeatedly as you trim the hide from the deer.

# 34

# HOW TO QUARTER A DEER IN 7 EASY STEPS

B utchering your deer at home can often seem like a daunting task. The reality is that making this "job" into a convenient and fun project requires managing the size of the portions of meat with which you work. Quartering your deer will enable you to work with smaller and controllable portions within a limited area.

Many hunters think quartering a deer requires a lot of expensive butchering tools and additional time and work. This is simply not the case. With just a quality knife, sharpening steel and a small saw, anyone can quarter a deer at home and remove its front and hind quarters, tenderloins, ribs and backstraps by following these simple step-by-step directions.

Begin by hanging the deer by the neck or head, positioned so that you are cutting at a comfortable height.

## STEP # 1

Push the front leg away from the deer's skinned carcass. Using a sharp hunting or butchering knife, place the blade sharp edge down and cut the connective meat and tissue free from between the leg and the rib cage. Continue cutting this section until you reach the shoulder. This process is easier if someone holds the carcass steady in a safe position as you cut it. Otherwise, you can tie the opposite leg to an anchor point to help steady the carcass.

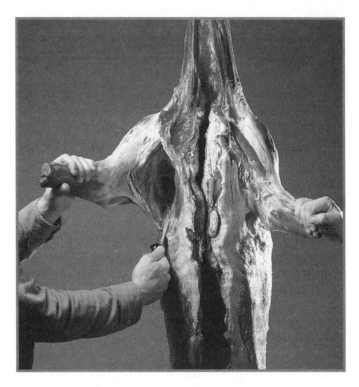

The layers of muscle can be used as a guide to help make removing sections of meat much easier. Here you can see how there is a natural separation of the shoulder from the carcass. (photo CPi)

## STEP # 2

When you have cut the front leg and are at the shoulder, remove it by cutting between the shoulder blade and the back. Repeat steps one and two on the opposite front leg. Once both legs are off, remove the layer of brisket meat that is located over the deer's ribs.

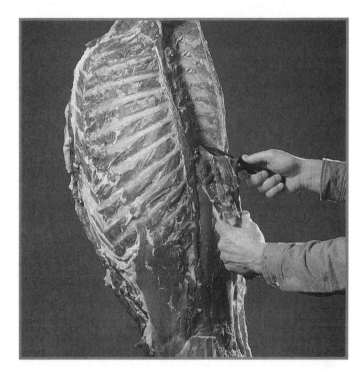

The back straps are some of the most prized cuts of meat. Be careful when removing them. Use the spine as a guide and it will help to minimize the number of tasty bits of the back strap left on the deer. (photo CPi)

## STEP # 3

Now, cut the meat at the base of the neck, which will allow you to cut out the backstraps. On one side of the spine, with the knife blade facing down and the tip of blade pressed closely to the bone, guide the knife slowly down toward the rump of the deer. Be extra careful not to cut into the backstrap and leave any of its prime meat behind. Once you reach the rump area, cut off the backstrap. Repeat on the other side of the spine.

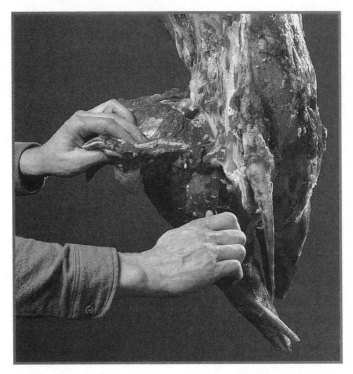

As when you are skinning a deer, make sure the carcass is at a level that offer you the most comfort and best leverage to make your cuts. (photo CPi)

## STEP # 4

Next, cut one of the hind legs off, which will expose the ball-and-socket joint. Push the leg back forcefully until the joint pops apart. Now cut through the joint. Carefully work your knife around the tailbone and pelvis area until the leg becomes free. Repeat this step on the opposite rear leg.

## STEP # 5

After trimming away the flank meat below the last rib, it is time to cut the tenderloins from the inside of the deer's body cavity. They are smaller than the loins, located on the underside of the spine.

Don't forget to remove one of the most delectable cuts of deer - the tenderloins. They are found on the inside of the ribs. (photo CPi)

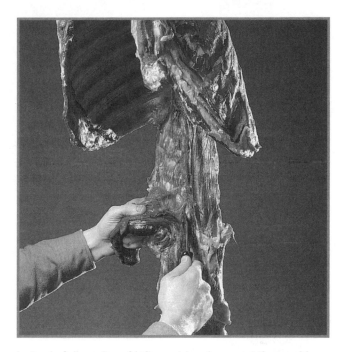

Instead of disposing of leftover trimmings - set them aside as you butcher the deer. You'll be happily surprised to see how much leftover meat will accumulate. It can be used for ground venison for burgers or sausage. (photo CPi)

## STEP # 6

To remove the ribs, simply saw along the backbone of the deer, cut around the base of the neck, and snap off the backbone. Set aside the neck and head. Carefully bone-out as much usable meat from the neck as possible. It makes terrific chopped meat or it can be rolled as a pot roast.

## STEP # 7

To enhance the taste and tenderness of the ribs, carefully trim away all the gristle, fat and ridge located at the bottom of the rib sections. It you want to make the ribs into short ribs, saw them in half. If you prefer not to eat the ribs, don't discard them! Instead, bone the meat from the surrounding ribs and grind it into sausage or burger meat.

To save the ribs, which are highly prized cuts of meat, remove the spine and any leftover fat or connective tissue. (photo CPi)

## DID YOU KNOW ...?

• The flank meat is often used to make jerky. It can be ground for burger meat as well.

• By removing the tenderloins before properly aging your deer, you will prevent them from turning black and dehydrating and also dramatically increase their flavor and tenderness.

• The primary cause of bad-tasting game meat is from the "silverskin"—the shiny, silky-looking connective tissue—and the tallow (fat). The fat from domestic animals imparts flavor to their meat, but that's not the case with wild animals—especially antlered game. Remove every piece of silverskin and tallow you see to avoid "gamey"-tasting venison. It is a time consuming process, but well worth the extra effort.

# CLOSING THOUGHTS

While working on our first book, Peter and I had enough projects to fill two books. Thanks to the Archery Trade Association—who expressed a desire for a DIY project book—we were able to focus those ideas on projects for the archer.

We also wanted more than just a DIY book for making projects; we wanted to share Peter's vast knowledge of hunting, as well as some tricks of the trade with the bowhunters of America.

So here it is; a book that has some nice, useful projects for the camp, home, or farm. You can hunt from them, hang them on your wall, move and store your equipment, hang or display your trophies, hang your bow, display your archery equipment, provide an organized place to work, improve your archery skills, and learn how easy it is to make some unusual projects from bone, rack, unused archery equipment, and even have some fun with games.

It has been an exciting and fun project. The time spent in my workshop provided me with hours of enjoyment and anticipation. Many times I envisioned readers stepping back from a project they built and feeling a sense of pride and satisfaction - those thoughts helped me to stay up late at night completing these projects.

Both Peter and I know you will not only enjoy making these woodworking projects but will also get a lot of real-life use out of each and every one of them. We hope once you complete several of the projects in the book, you will be motivated to start buying more tools and take on even more woodworking jobs - maybe even some of your own design ideas as well.

Thanks to all of you for purchasing this book and we hope that you enjoy it enough that we will have to write a "part-two" for you! Good woodworking in the meantime.

Stay tuned for our next book, we are already thinking of the great projects we know you will enjoy.

*Leo Somma and Peter Fiduccia*

# APPENDIX A

# SILENT SHADOW ARCHERY WINDOW

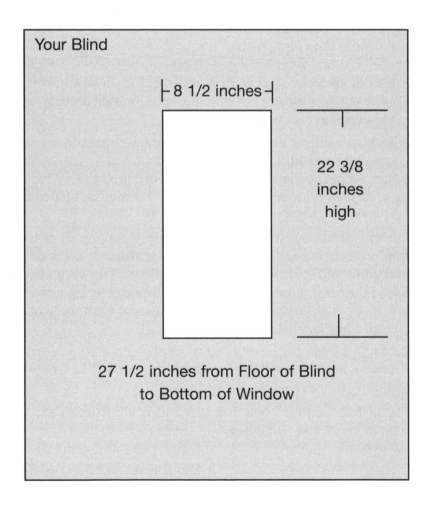

Your Blind

8 1/2 inches

22 3/8 inches high

27 1/2 inches from Floor of Blind to Bottom of Window

**Materials & Tools:** Cordless drill, square drive bit (for screws), saws all or saber saw, ruler, level, hand or air staple gun (to put screws in velcro strap), and a can of aerosol Rustoleum paint (to paint shield and parts) in your choice of color.

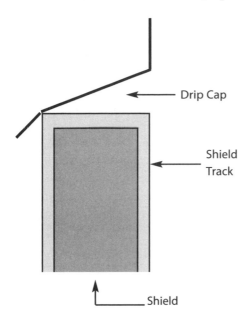

Drip Cap

Shield Track

Shield

**Step #1** - The measurements on the previous page are for cutting holes in your blind walls, in order to install your window kit. You can center, or offset, the openings to put two windows side by side, setting them about 2 feet apart (depending on the side of your wall). Cut the openings for the windows.

**Step #2** - Install the outside shield track and shield stop screws.

A. On the 22 3/8-inch height side, measure over 1 5/8 inches. Be sure to measure over top and bottom on both sides.

B. Hold the Shield Channel down on the line at the top hole, raise the channel about 1/8-inch above the top of the window and secure it with a screw. Make sure you align the channel with both marks.

C. Fasten the channel with two additional screws. Repeat on the left side.

D. Install the bottom Z Channel, overlapping the top Z Channel. use a small level to get the long track straight. Measure down from the top of the upper Z 45 1/2 inches to the bottom of lower Z.

E. Install the stop screws on both shield tracks.

**Step #3** - Install the Shield

Drop in the shield (rivets to the bottom) making sure you have enough clearance so the shield slides up and down smoothly.

**Step #4 -** Install the Drip Cap

It is critical to set the Drip Cap on top of the Shield Track, as seen in the line drawing (on page 253). Put in one screw on the right side. Set the Drip Cap on the left and screw fast. Finish screwing the Drip Cap in place. Put additional screws between the holes in the Drip Cap.

**Step #5 -** Staple the Velcro to the Inside of Your Blind

A. Pull the shield up and down a few times to get the strap to the center in the window. Once you have found the center, let the shield down and staple the loop part onto the wall of your blind, starting at the bottom of the strap.

B. Put two staples side by side at the bottom of the strap so that the corners of the velcro won't turn up.

C. After stapling the velcro strap, the shield installation is complete. Repeat this step on the remaining windows.

Step #6 - Install the Glass Track & Velcro Strap Spacers

A. Remove the paper from the glass. Slide the foam glass track on each side of the glass panel.

B. Stall the wooden strap spacer. use a hand stapler or air stapler to install. This has to be installed to allow the strap to move freely.

C. To install the glass track, start by holding the bottom of the glass track on the top of the strap spacer. Hold the window even in opening and screw in on the right side. Make sure the track is level and secure it on the left side. Repeat at the top, making sure the glass slides smoothly.

D. To install the stop screw (screw with the rubber sleeve), open the glass so it opens past the window opening by about one-half inch and screw in the screw. Repeat on other windows.

(Author's note: Additional photo support for these steps can be found at www.shadowhunterllc.com)

# APPENDIX B

# SOURCES FOR MATERIALS
# AND SUPPLIES

84 Lumber
We dealt with various store locations so here is their
Web site: www.84-lumber.com

Camo Blind Wrap
www.omnova.com
Shadow Hunter LLC
www.shadowhunterllc.com
22724 96th Avenue
Marcellus, MI 49067
(888) 446-4868 or (269) 646-9189

E-Z KUT Hunting Products
www.ezkutpruners.com
1935 S. Plum Grove Rd. Suite 355
Palatine, IL 60067
(847) 253-8537

The Home Depot
We dealt with various store locations so here is their
Web site: www.homedepot.com

Lowe's Home Improvement
We dealt with various store locations so here is their
Web site: www.lowes.com

Riverhead Building Supply Corporation
www.rbscorp.com
165 West Montauk Highway
Hampton Bays, NY 11946
(631) 728-0307

Southern Outdoor Technologies, LLC
www.southernoutdoortechnologies.com
P.O. Box 1135
801 W. Churchill Rd.
West Point, MS 39779
(662) 295-5702

Tractor Supply Company,
www.mytscstore.com
5640 State Hwy. 12
Norwich, NY 13815
(607)336-8811

## Local Hardware and Paint Stores

Butternut Valley Hardware Co.
18 Marion Ave.
Gilbertsville, NY 13776
(607) 783-2291

Paint Wall Paper Express Limited
216 W Montauk Highway
Hampton Bays, NY 11946
(631) 728-5701

Shinnecock Hardware, Inc
91 W Montauk Hwy
Hampton Bays, NY 11946
(631) 728-4602

# APPENDIX C

# RECOMMENDED READING

*25 Projects for Outdoorsmen: Quick and Easy Plans for Deer Camp, Home, Woods, and Backyard*, The Lyons Press, 2007, Peter J. Fiduccia and Leo Somma

*Backyard Structures and How to Buld Them,* The Lyons Press, 2005, Monte Burch

*Basic Woodworking: All the Skills and Tools You Need to Get Started* Stackpole Books, 2004, Cheryl Sobun, editor

Black & Decker: *Quick and Easy Weekend Woodworking Projects* Popular Woodworking Books, 2005, The editors of Popular Woodworking

Black & Decker: *Workshops You Can Build,* Firefly Books, 2005, David Stiles and Jeanie Stiles

*The Complete Guide to Easy Woodworking Projects,* Creative Publishing international, 2003

*The Home Cabinetmaker: Woodworking Techniques, Furniture Building,* and Installing Millwork, Popular Science, 1987, Monte Burch

*HomeMade:101 Easy-to-Make Things For Your Garden, Home, or Farm,* Storey Publishing, LLC, 1980, Ken Braren & Roger Griffith

*How to Build Treehouses, Huts, and Forts,* The Lyons Press, 2003, David Stiles

*Popular Woodworking: Complete Book of Tips, Tricks, & Techniques* Popular Woodworking Books, 2004, The editors of Popular Woodworking

*Sheds, Gazebos & Outbuildings*, Creative Publishing international, 2002

SAVE OUR HERITAGE

# SAVE OUR HERITAGE
## "Your Investment in the Future of Archery and Bowhunting"

The Save Our Heritage initiative comes from the Archery Trade Association and the Bowhunting Preservation Alliance. With the purchase of this book, you are supporting programs that help grow the sports you love–archery and bowhunting. SOH book proceeds support community archery programs and parks; archery range building and refurbishing in-school and after-school archery and bowhunting programs; and many more nationwide efforts to grow archery and protect and promote bowhunting.

## DID YOU KNOW?

★ The ATA has invested and pledged nearly $2 million to bring introductory archery and bowhunting programs and shooting facilities to U.S. cities, while the group also works to sustain and grow bowhunting.

★ ATA continues to expand their community archery strategy as part of its work to make archery a mainstream sport. Alabama, Florida, South Dakota, Nebraska, Iowa, Nevada, Tennessee, Arizona, New Jersey, Michigan, Minnesota, and Alaska are examples of states where funding is used for new archery programs and archery parks, shooting facilities, and archery ranges.

★ ATA partners with state wildlife agencies to fund archery or shooting program coordinators who lead community archery strategies on the local level.

★ ATA paid for a research study that analyzed the effectiveness of school archery programs and printed a brochure, <u>Archery, the Safe Sport</u>, summarizing the results. The brochure helps administrators and others understand the value of school archery programs.

★ ATA's brochure, <u>Archery, the Safe Sport</u>, is an invaluable tool when discussing the safety aspects of archery with school and recreation program administrators.

★ ATA created *Explore Bowhunting*, a curriculum designed to help instructors, program leaders and educators teach students ages 11-17 the basic skills of bowhunting, while engaging them in the outdoors.

★ ATA completed 24 *Explore Bowhunting* pilot programs in five states during the 2008-09 school year to fine-tune lesson plans and test the effectiveness of its goals. Beginning in 2010, the curriculum began launching in select states across the country.

★ ATA works with state agencies to develop urban deer hunting opportunities.

★ ATA partnered with the U.S. Fish and Wildlife Service to offer more bowhunting opportunities on the National Wildlife Refuges.

★ ATA has provided legal defense for private landowners whose right to bowhunt has been challenged by neighbors, local groups or even residential associations.

**Thank you! Your support of the Save Our Heritage program provides funds for these programs . . . and more.**

LOOKING FOR AN ARCHERY RETAILER?

# ARCHERYSEARCH ◎ COM

LOOKING FOR AN ARCHERY INSTRUCTOR?

# ARCHERYSEARCH ◎ COM

LOOKING FOR AN ARCHERY RANGE?

# ARCHERYSEARCH ◎ COM

LOOKING FOR AN ARCHERY CLUB?

# ARCHERYSEARCH ◎ COM

Where you'll find all the answers to your archery and bowhunting questions

# NOTES

**DO-IT-YOURSELF PROJECTS FOR BOWHUNTERS**

_____
_____
_____
_____
_____
_____
_____
_____
_____
_____
_____
_____
_____
_____
_____
_____
_____
_____
_____
_____
_____
_____
_____
_____
_____
_____
_____
_____
_____
_____
_____
_____
_____
_____
_____
_____

## DO-IT-YOURSELF PROJECTS FOR BOWHUNTERS

_____
_____
_____
_____
_____
_____
_____
_____
_____
_____
_____
_____
_____
_____
_____
_____
_____
_____
_____
_____
_____
_____
_____
_____
_____
_____
_____
_____
_____
_____
_____
_____
_____
_____
_____